SWU-NAP- 019

UNIFORMS OF RUSSIAN ARMY DURING THE NAPOLEONIC WAR VOL.14

UNDER THE REIGN OF ALEXANDER I
EMPEROR OF RUSSIA BETWEEN 1801 AND 1825
GARRISONS, INVALIDS, MEDICAL & VETERINARY CORPS

From the Viskovatov's greatest work:
"Historical description of the clothing and
arms of the Russian Army"

English translation by Mark Conrad

SOLDIERSHOP PUBLISHING

AUTHOR

Aleksandr Vasilevich Viskovatov born 22 April (4 May New Style) 1804, died 27 February (11 March) 1858 in St. Petersburg, Russian military historian. He graduated from the 1st Cadet Corps and served in the artillery, the hydrographic depot of the Naval Ministry, and then in the Department of Military Educational Institutions. He mainly studied historical artifacts and the histories of military units. Viskovatov's greatest work was the Historical Description of the Clothing and Arms of the Russian Army.

PUBLISHING'S NOTE

NOTE ABOUT BOOK PRINTING BEFORE 1925

LICENSES COMMONS

ACKNOWLEDGEMENTS

A Special Thanks to NYPL and other institutions for their kindly permission to use some images of his archives, collections or books used in our book.

Title: **UNIFORMS OF RUSSIAN ARMY DURING THE NAPOLEONIC WAR VOL. 14**
Garrisons, Invalids, Medical & Veterinary Corps
By A.V.Viskovatov. Serie edit by Luca S. Cristini. First edition by Soldiershop. January 2018
Cover & Art Design: Luca S. Cristini. Plates re-colorations by Anna Cristini.
ISBN code: 978-88-93273053
Published by Soldiershop publishing, via Padre Davide, 7 - 24050 Zanica (BG) ITALY. www.soldiershop.com

SOLDIERSHOP
PUBLISHING
BOOK on DEMAND

UNIFORMS OF THE RUSSIAN ARMY DURING THE NAPOLEONIC WAR VOL. 14

UNDER THE REIGN OF ALEXANDER I EMPEROR OF RUSSIA BETWEEN 1801 AND 1825

*

GARRISONS, INVALIDS, MEDICAL & VETERINARY CORPS

Russian uniforms of Alexander Czar's era 1818 about

HISTORICAL DESCRIPTION OF THE CLOTHING AND ARMS OF THE RUSSIAN ARMY - A.V. VISKOVATOV

(First English translation by Mark Conrad)

Soldiershop is glad to presents the complete collection of the great job made by A.V. Viskovatov dedicated to the uniforms and weapons belonging to the Russian army during the Napoleonic period, until 1825. The time we considered corresponds to the reigns of two Tzars: Paul I, who reigned since 1769 until his murder on the 23rd of March 1801, and his son Aleksandr Pavlovič Romanov, that with the title of Alexander I, sat on the throne until the 1st December 1825.

Our reprint in based on the original 19th century volumes, to be precise the volumes from 7 to 9 are dedicated to the reign of Paul I; this first part is distributed on 7 volumes, having a numbering from 1 to 7. From number 10 to 18 of the original volumes, the second part is dedicated to the Russian troops under Alexander I. These still being worked on and they will be soon ready, distributed on twenty volumes approximately. Our new edition, the first ever published in English, both on paper and digital format, boasts a large number of color plates, many of them unpublished and coloured by our team of expert artists and scholars of uniformology. Each volume is based on 50/70 plates, always accompanied by the original translated text which describes the uniforms, the organization and the armament of the Russian army of the period.

A unique work in its genre, a must have in any respecting collection!

Aleksandr Vasilevich Viskovatov born 22 April (4 May New Style) 1804, died 27 February (11 March) 1858 in St. Petersburg, Russian military historian. He graduated from the 1st Cadet Corps and served in the artillery, the hydrographic depot of the Naval Ministry, and then in the Department of Military Educational Institutions.

He mainly studied historical artifacts and the histories of military units. Viskovatov's greatest work was the Historical Description of the Clothing and Arms of the Russian Army (Vols. 1-30, St. Petersburg, 1841-62; 2nd ed. Vols. 1-34, St. Petersburg - Novosibirsk - Leningrad, 1899-1948). This work is based on a great quantity of archival documents and contains four thousand colored illustrations.

Viskovatov was the author of Chronicles of the Russian Army (Books 1-20, St. Petersburg, 1834-42) and Chronicles of the Russian Imperial Army (Parts 1-7, St. Petersburg, 1852). He collected valuable material on the history of the Russian navy which went into A Short Overview of Russian Naval Campaigns and General Voyages to the End of the XVII Century (St. Petersburg, 1864; 2nd edition Moscow, 1946). Together with A.I. Mikhailovskii-Danilevskii he helped prepare and create the Military Gallery in the Winter Palace.

He wrote the historical military inscriptions for the walls of the Hall of St. George in the Great Palace of the Kremlin. (From the article in the Soviet Military Encyclopedia.)

CONTENTS

*

RUSSIAN ARMY- GARRISONS, INTERNAL GUARD, INVALIDS, RECRUITS, ADMINISTRATIVE OFFICIALS, AND MEDICAL AND VETERINARY PERSONNEL.

CHANGES IN THE UNIFORMS AND EQUIPMENT OF GARRISONS, THE INTERNAL GUARD, INVALIDS, MILITARY ORPHANS' DETACHMENTS, MILITARY CANTONIST DETACHMENTS, PROVINCIAL COMPANIES, STATE COMMANDS, MINES BATTALIONS, RECRUITS, AND OFFICIALS IN THE MILITARY ADMINISTRATION WHO DO NOT BELONG TO TROOP UNITS, FROM 1801 TO 1825:

XVII. GARRISON REGIMENTS AND BATTALIONS
[*Garnizonnye polki i bataliony*]

9 April 1801 - Lower ranks of Garrison units were ordered to cut off their **curls** [*pukli*] and have **queues** [*kosy*] only 4 vershoks [7 inches] long, tying them midway down the collar (1).

15 January 1802 – New rule were established for the pattern and sewing of **uniform coats** for combatant and noncombatant, or lower staff [*unter-shtabnyi*], ranks (2).

17 March 1802 – Supplementary rules were confirmed regarding patterns for **garrison uniforms** (3).

30 April 1802 - Confirmation was given to a new **table of uniforms, accouterments, and weapons** for garrison regiments and battalions, based upon which, as well as on the preceding directives, *privates of Garrisons on a field establishment* [*polevoe polozhenie*], were prescribed all uniform clothing and weapons as for privates in musketeer regiments at this time, i.e. coat [*mundir*] or caftan [*kaftan*], pants [*pantalony*], boots [*sapogi*], neckcloth [*galstuk*], hats [*shlyapyi*], forage cap [*furazhnaya shapka*], greatcoat [*shinel'*], warm coat [*fufaika*]; sword [*shpaga*] with short-sword blade [*tesachnyi klinok*], swordknot [*temlyak*], swordbelt [*portupeya*], musket [*ruzh'e*] with bayonet [*shtyk*], pouch [*suma*] with crossbelt [*perevyaz'*]; knapsack [*ranets*], and water flask [*vodonosnaya flyazha*]. The only differences were that buttons were white, the pouch had no badge, and the color of the collar, lapels, and shoulder straps were in accordance with the list presented below (Illus. 1773) (4).

Noncommissioned officers were uniformed the same as privates but with only one shoulder strap, on the right shoulder, with silver galloon on the coat's collar and cuffs. Tassels on the hat were in three colors: white, black, and orange. Like noncommisioned officers in Army Infantry regiments, they did not wear pouches and had gloves, canes, a sword belt without a bayonet frog, and halberds (Illus. 1774). Only officer candidates [*podpraporshchiki*], of which there were two in a battalion, were not prescribed to have these last items (Illus. 1775) (5).

Company, *battalion*, and *regimental drummers* had the same distinctions as prescribed for these reanks in Army infantry regiments (Illus. 1776 and 1777) (6).

Company-grade officers, adjutants, field-grade officers, and *Generals* were uniformed exactly the same as in Army infantry but without gorgets (Illus. 1778, 1779, and 1780) (7).

Noncombatant lower ranks were uniformed as the corresponding ranks in Army infantry (Illus. 1781 and 1782) (8).

Doctors and *Auditors* were prescribed the existing standard uniforms for these ranks, as described in detail above for grenadier regiments (9).

In Garrisons on an internal establishment, privates carried bayonets instead of swords. Otherwise, all uniform clothing and weapons for these Garrisons were the same as those authorized for Garrisons on a field establishment (10).

6 July 1802 – A list of colors for privates' hat tassels was confirmed. Based on this, and the orders of 17 March and the table of 30 April, cited above, Garrisons were prescibed the following (11):

Finland Inspection

Viborg Regiment: Yellow collar and cuffs; red shoulder straps; hat tassels – 1st Battalion white with a red center; 2nd Battalion red; halberd and spontoon shafts and drumsticks straw-colored (Illlus. 1773).

Fredrikshamn Regiment: Yellow collar and cuffs; white shoulder straps; hat tassels – 1st Battalion white, 2nd Battalion red with a white center; halberd and spontoon shafts and drumsticks white.

Rochensalm Regiment: Yellow collar, cuffs, and shoulder straps; hat tassels – 1st Battalion white with a rose center, 2nd Battalion yellow with a rose center, 3rd Battaloin red with a rose center; halberd and spontoon shafts and drumsticks coffee-colored.

Villmanstrand Battalion: Yellow collar and cuffs; light-raspberry shoulder straps; hat tassels white with a yellow center; halberd and spontoon shafts and drumsticks white.

Kexholm Battalion: Yellow collar and cuffs; turquoise shoulder straps; hat tassels white with a light-raspberry center; halberd and spontoon shafts and drumsticks coffee-colored.

Nyslott Battalion: Yellow collar and cuffs; rose shoulder straps; hat tassels white with a turquoise center; halberd and spontoon shafts and drumsticks straw-colored.

St.-Petersburg Inspection

Kronstadt Regiment: Red collar, cuffs, and shoulder straps; hat tassels – 1st Battalion white with a red center; 2nd Battalion sky blue with a red center, 3rd Battalion green with a red center, 4th Battalion red; halberd and spontoon shafts and drumsticks coffee-colored (Illlus. 1774).

Narva Battalion: Red collar and cuffs; white shoulder straps; hat tassels white with a yellow center; halberd and spontoon shafts and drumsticks white.

Novgorod Battalion: Red collar and cuffs, yellow shoulder straps; hat tassels white with a raspberry center; halberd and spontoon shafts and drumsticks white.

Pskov Battalion: Red collar and cuffs; light-raspberry shoulder straps; hat tassels white with a turquoise center; halberd and spontoon shafts and drumsticks black.

Schlüsselburg Battalion: Red collar and cuffs; turquoise shoulder straps; hat tassels white; halberd and spontoon shafts and drumsticks white.

Lifland Inspectorate:

Riga Regiment: Turqoise collar and cuffs; red shoulder straps; hat tassels – 1st Battalion white with a red center; 2nd Battalion sky blue with a red center, 3rd Battalion green with a red center, 4th Battalion red; halberd and spontoon shafts and drumsticks black (Illlus. 1775).

Dünamünde Battalion: Turquoise collar and cuffs; yellow shoulder straps; hat tassels white with a yellow center; halberd and spontoon shafts and drumsticks white.

Pernau Battalion: Turquoise collar and cuffs, light-raspberry shoulder straps; hat tassels white; halberd and spontoon shafts and drumsticks coffee-colored.

Arensburg Battalion: Turquoise collar, cuffs, and shoulder straps; hat tassels white with a turquoise center; halberd and spontoon shafts and drumsticks black.

Dniester Inspectorate:

Kherson Regiment: Lilac collar and cuffs; red shoulder straps; hat tassels – 1st Battalion white with a red center; 2nd Battalion red; halberd and spontoon shafts and drumsticks white (Illlus. 1776).

Ochakov Battalion: Lilac collar and cuffs; white shoulder straps; hat tassels white; halberd and spontoon shafts and drumsticks white.

Crimea Inspectorate:

Akhtiar Regiment: Flesh-colored [*blanzhevyi*] collar and cuffs; red shoulder straps; hat tassels – 1st Battalion white; 2nd Battalion red with a white center; halberd and spontoon shafts and drumsticks white.

Perekop Battalion: Flesh-colored collar and cuffs; white shoulder straps; hat tassels white with a red center; halberd and spontoon shafts and drumsticks black.

Caucasus Inspectorate:

Astrakhan Regiment: Dark-blue collar and cuffs; red shoulder straps; hat tassels – 1st Battalion white with a red center; 2nd Battalion yellow with a red center, 3rd Battalion red; halberd and spontoon shafts and drumsticks black (Illus. 1777).

Dmitriev Regiment: Dark-blue collar and cuffs; white shoulder straps; hat tassels – 1st Battalion white, 2nd Battalion red with a white center; halberd and spontoon shafts and drumsticks straw-colored.

Tsaritsyn Battalion: Dark-blue collar and cuffs; yellow shoulder straps; hat tassels white with a yellow center; halberd and spontoon shafts and drumsticks white.

Azov Battalion: Dark-blue collar and cuffs; light-raspberry shoulder straps; hat tassels white with a light-raspberry center; halberd and spontoon shafts and drumsticks black.

Taganrog Battalion: Dark-blue collar and cuffs; turquoise shoulder straps; hat tassels white with a turquoise center; halberd and spontoon shafts and drumsticks straw-colored.

Mozdok Battalion: Dark-blue collar and cuffs; rose shoulder straps; hat tassels white with a light-green center; halberd and spontoon shafts and drumsticks black.

Kizlyar Regiment: Dark-blue collar and cuffs; light-green shoulder straps; hat tassels – 1st Battalion white with a rose center, 2nd Battalion red with a rose center; halberd and spontoon shafts and drumsticks black.

Smolensk Inspectorate:

Smolensk Battalion: White collar and cuffs; red shoulder straps; hat tassels white with a red center; halberd and spontoon shafts and drumsticks white (Illus. 1778).

Vitebsk Battalion: White collar, cuffs, and shoulder straps; hat tassels white; halberd and spontoon shafts and drumsticks straw-colored.

Mogilev Battalion: White collar and cuffs; yellow shoulder straps; hat tassels white with a yellow center; halberd and spontoon shafts and drumsticks white.

Kiev Inspectorate:

Kiev Regiment: Light-raspberry collar and cuffs; red shoulder straps; hat tassels – 1st Battalion white with a red center; 2nd Battalion red; halberd and spontoon shafts and drumsticks straw-colored (Illus. 1779).

Moscow Inspectorate:

Moscow Regiment: Orange collar and cuffs; red shoulder straps; hat tassels – 1st Battalion white with a red center; 2nd Battalion sky-blue with a red center, 3rd Battalion green with a red center, 4th Battalion red; halberd and spontoon shafts and drumsticks white (Illus. 1780).

Tver Battalion: Orange collar and cuffs; white shoulder straps; hat tassels white with a gray center; halberd and spontoon shafts and drumsticks black.

Vladimir Battalion: Orange collar and cuffs; yellow shoulder straps; hat tassels white with a rose center; halberd and spontoon shafts and drumsticks coffee-colored.

Nizhnii-Novgorod Battalion: Orange collar and cuffs; light-raspberry shoulder straps; hat tassels white with a light-green center; halberd and spontoon shafts and drumsticks white.

Tambov Battalion: Orange collar and cuffs; turquoise shoulder straps; hat tassels white with a light-raspberry center; halberd and spontoon shafts and drumsticks straw-colored.

Voronezh Battalion: Orange collar and cuffs; rose shoulder straps; hat tassels white; halberd and spontoon shafts and drumsticks straw-colored.

Saratov Battalion: Orange collar and cuffs; light-green shoulder straps; hat tassels white with a yellow center; halberd and spontoon shafts and drumsticks straw-colored.

Archangel Regiment: Orange collar and cuffs; gray shoulder straps; hat tassels – 1st Battalion white with a turquoise center, 2nd Battalion yellow with a turquoise center, 3rd Battalion red with a turquoise center; halberd and spontoon shafts and drumsticks black.

Orenburg Inspectorate:

Orenburg Regiment: Camel-colored collar and cuffs; red shoulder straps; hat tassels – 1st Battalion white; 2nd Battalion red with a white center; halberd and spontoon shafts and drumsticks black (Illus. 1781).

Kazan Regiment: Camel-colored collar and cuffs; white shoulder straps; hat tassels – 1st Battalion white with red center; 2nd Battalion red; halberd and spontoon shafts and drumsticks black.

Orsk Battalion: Camel-colored collar and cuffs; yellow shoulder straps; hat tassels white with a light-green center; halberd and spontoon shafts and drumsticks straw-colored.

Kizilsk Battalion: Camel-colored collar and cuffs; light-raspberry shoulder straps; hat tassels white with a yellow center; halberd and spontoon shafts and drumsticks white.

Verkhneuralsk Battalion: Camel-colored collar and cuffs; turquoise shoulder straps; hat tassels white with a light-raspberry center; halberd and spontoon shafts and drumsticks white.

Troitsk Battalion: Camel-colored collar and cuffs; rose shoulder straps; hat tassels white with a turquoise center; halberd and spontoon shafts and drumsticks black.

Zverinogolovsk Battalion: Camel-colored collar and cuffs; light-green shoulder straps; hat tassels white with a rose center; halberd and spontoon shafts and drumsticks black.

Simbirsk Battalion: Camel-colored collar and cuffs; gray shoulder straps; hat tassels white with a gray center; halberd and spontoon shafts and drumsticks black.

Siberia Inspectorate:

Tobolsk Regiment: Gray collar and cuffs; red shoulder straps; hat tassels – 1st Battalion white with a yellow center; 2nd Battalion red with a yellow center; halberd and spontoon shafts and drumsticks coffee-colored (Illus. 1782).

Tara Battalion: Gray collar and cuffs; white shoulder straps; hat tassels white with a dark-blue center; halberd and spontoon shafts and drumsticks white.

Omsk Battalion: Gray collar and cuffs; yellow shoulder straps; hat tassels white with a light-raspberry center; halberd and spontoon shafts and drumsticks white.

Petrovsk Battalion: Gray collar and cuffs; light-raspberry shoulder straps; hat tassels white with a turquoise center; halberd and spontoon shafts and drumsticks white.

Semipalatinsk Battalion: Gray collar and cuffs; turquoise shoulder straps; hat tassels white with a rose center; halberd and spontoon shafts and drumsticks black.

Zhelezinsk Battalion: Gray collar and cuffs; rose shoulder straps; hat tassels white with a rose center; halberd and spontoon shafts and drumsticks black.

Biisk Battalion: Gray collar and cuffs; light-green shoulder straps; hat tassels white with a light-green center; halberd and spontoon shafts and drumsticks white.

Irkutsk Regiment: Gray collar, cuffs, and shoulder straps; hat tassels – 1st Battalion white with a red center, 2nd Battalion yellow with a red center, 3rd Battalion red; halberd and spontoon shafts and drumsticks black.

Selenginsk Regiment: Gray collar and cuffs; lilac shoulder straps; hat tassels – 1st Battalion white, 2nd Battalion red with a white center; halberd and spontoon shafts and drumsticks straw-colored.

Kamchatka Battalion: Gray collar and cuffs; dark-blue shoulder straps; hat tassels white with a gray center; halberd and spontoon shafts and drumsticks white.

19 August 1803 – Lower ranks in all garrison regiments and battalions were given *shakos* in place of hats, of the same pattern as those received by lower ranks in musketeer regiments at this time, i.e. cloth with an affixed visor, small tassels as were on the hats (Illus. 1783), and cloth ear flaps for winter (12).

19 October 1803 - Noncommissioned officers of garrison regiments and battalions were ordered to have **two shoulder straps** instead of one (13).

1 July 1804 – Field and company-grade officers of garrison regiments were ordered to have shabracks and holsters with silver galloon, according to the pattern confirmed on 29 June 1803 for field and company-grade officers' shabracks and holsters in grenadier and musketeer regiments. In this same year officers' hats were ordered to be have a buttonhole loop of narrow silver galloon with a high plume (Illus. No 1783) (14).

3 August 1804 – **Newly formed garrison battalions** were prescribed to have collars, cuffs, and shoulder straps of the following colors:

Mitau – (St.-Petersburg Inspectorate) red collar and cuffs, rose shoulder straps.

Grodno – (Lithuania Inspectorate) light-green collar and cuffs, red shoulder straps.

Vilna – (Lithuania Inspectorate) light-green collar and cuffs, white shoulder straps.

Minsk – (Lithuania Inspectorate) light-green collar and cuffs, yellow shoulder straps.

Vladikavkaz – (Caucasus Inspectorate) dark-blue collar and cuffs, gray shoulder straps.

Yekaterinoslav – (Kiev Inspectorate) light-raspberry collar and cuffs, white shoulder straps.

Velikii-Ustyug – (Moscow Inspectorate) orange collar and cuffs, lilac shoulder straps.

Vologda – (Moscow Inspectorate) orange collar and cuffs, dark-blue shoulder straps.

Vyatka – (Orenburg Inspectorate) camel-colored collar and cuffs, lilac shoulder straps.

Ufa – (Orenburg Inspectorate) camel-colored collar and cuffs, dark-blue shoulder straps (15).

31 December 1804 – The *Kherson*Garrison Regiment and *Ochakov* Garrison Battalion that belonged to the Dniester Inspectorate were ordered to have: dark-green collars and cuff flaps, with red piping; red cuffs; shoulder straps of the previous colors, i.e. Kherson – red, Ochakov – white (Illus. 1783) (16).

15 January 1805 – The four garrison battalions newly established on the **Orenburg Line** under the name of *Orenburg Line Battalions* were ordered to have camel-colored collars and cuffs, i.e. the color prescribed for the Orenburg Inspectorate, while shoulder straps were camel-colored in the 1st (*Verkhneozernaya*), orange in the 2nd (*Orsk*), straw-colored in the 4th (*Verkhneuralsk*), and black in the 4th (*Troitsk*) (17).

19 January 1805 – In order to more clearly differentiate personnel of the various regiments and battalions in the **Caucasus Inspectorate** when they were in **forage caps**, it was permitted to sew a cloth ribbon around the upper edge of the cap band, of the regimental color—i.e. that prescribed for shoulder straps—and 1/2 vershok [7/8 inch] wide, leaving the cap band trim visible above it (18).

23 December 1805 — To obviate the inconveniences often met with when in battle with the enemy, Generals and field and company-grade officers of units in the **Caucasus Inspectorate**, including the Kizlyar, Mozdok, and Vladikavkaz Garrisons, were permitted, instead of hats, to wear *shakos*, similar throughout to those of the soldiers except with a silver pompon with a mix of black and orange silk instead of a woolen tassel. These shakos were authorized only for campaigns and military operations, and during other times hats were to be worn (19).

5 January 1806 – For the newly established *Penza Garrison Battalion* (Moscow Inspectorate), collars and cuffs were prescribed to be orange and shoulder straps camel-colored (20).

1 July 1806 – Changes in the uniforms of **garrison doctors** were ordered, similar to those described above for Army infantry regiments (21).

20 August 1806 – **Collars** and **cuffs** in all garrison regiments and battalions were ordered to be yellow, and shoulder straps and skirt and turnback lining to be red (Illus. 1784). The shoulder straps were to be with numbers of white worsted cord according to the list below:

Riga Regiment – 1	Kazan Regiment – 18
Reval Regiment – 2	Moscow Regiment – 19
Dünamünde Battalion – 3	Tver Battalion – 20
Pernau Battalion – 4	Vladimir Battalion – 21
Arensburg Battalion – 5	Nizhnii-Novgorod Battalion – 22
Mitau Battalion – 6	Vyatka Battalion – 23
Kronstadt Regiment – 7	Velikii-Ustyug Battalion – 24
Narva Battalion – 8	Vologda Battalion – 25
Schlüsselburg Battalion – 9	Archangel Regiment – 26
Novgorod Battalion – 10	Simbirsk Battalion – 27
Pskov Battalion – 11	Voronezh Battalion – 28
Viborg Regiment - 12	Saratov Battalion – 29
Fredrikshamn Regiment - 13	Tsaritsyn Battalion – 30
Rochensalm Regiment - 14	Astrakhan Regiment – 31
Villmanstrand Battalion – 15	Kizlyar Regiment – 32
Kexholm Battalion – 16	Mozdok Battalion – 33
Nyslott Battalion – 17	Vladikavkaz Regiment – 34

Azov Battalion – 35	Kizilsk Battalion – 54
Dimitrii Regiment – 36	Verkhneuralsk Battalion – 55
Taganrog Battalion – 37	Troitsk Battalion – 56
Perekop Battalion – 38	Zverinogolovsk Battalion – 57
Akhtiar Battalion – 39	Orsk Battalion – 58
Kherson Regiment – 40	1st Orenburg Line Battalion – 59
Ochakov Battalion – 41	2nd Orenburg Line Battalion – 60
Yekaterinoslav Battalion – 42	3rd Orenburg Line Battalion – 61
Kiev Regiment – 43	4th Orenburg Line Battalion – 62
Mogilev Battalion – 44	Tomsk (formerly Tara) – 63
Vitebsk Battalion – 45	Omsk Regiment – 64
Smolensk Battalion – 46	Petrovsk Battalion – 65
Minsk Battalion – 47	Semipalatinsk Battalion – 66
Grodno Battalion – 48	Biisk Battalion – 67
Vilna Battalion – 49	Zhelezinsk Battalion – 68
Tambov Battalion – 50	Tobolsk Regiment – 69
Penza Battalion – 51	Irkutsk Regiment – 70
Ufa Battalion – 52	Selenginsk Regiment – 71
Orenburg Regiment – 53	Kamchatka Battalion – 72 (22)

2 December 1806 — Lower ranks were ordered to cut their **hair** short; Generals and field and company-grade officers, however, were in this case allowed to proceed according to their personal inclination (23).

10 March 1807 — Officers' **spontoons** were abolished, and in their place it was ordered that they use **swords** [*shpagi*] while in formation (24).

23 December 1807 — Lower ranks in all garrison regiments and battalions were given **summer and winter pants** and boots according to the patterns confirmed at this time for Army infantry regiments, i.e. the first with spats and the second with leather cuffs provided with seven white (tinned) buttons (Illus. 1785) (25).

8 March 1808 – In garrison regiments and battalions **swordbelts** were ordered to be worn over the shoulder as laid down on 19 December 1807 for Army Infantry regiments, and from this time forward the previous headdress or kiver began to be trimmed with leather and made with sewn-on visors (Illus. 1785) (26).

16 May 1808 – Garrison Generals and field and company-grade officers were ordered to have *epaulettes* of the same pattern as confirmed on 17 September 1807 for army General and officers, except of silver with a red cloth field and a number in silver thin cord (Illus. 1786) (27).

5 August 1808 – For all garrison regiments and battalions, it was ordered to issue madder red cloth [*sukno krashenoe krapom*] for the lining of coattails and any similar place that was had been prescribed to be bright red (28).

2 November 1808 - The **summer and winter pants** authorized on 23 December 1807 were kept only for combatant lower ranks, while for noncombatants the pants, as well as boots, were directed to be of the patterns introduced in 1802 (29).

5 December 1808 – In all garrison regiments and battalions **halberd shafts** as well as the corresponding **drumsticks** were ordered to be of a single color—coffee (30).

22 January 1808 – The rules established on 26 January 1808 for Generals in grenadier, musketeer, and other army regiments regarding when they were to be regimental uniform and when in the standard **general-officer's coat** were extended to garrison Generals, with the only difference being that for the latter, embroidery, buttons, and epaulettes were to be silver instead of gold (31).

11 February 1809 – In garrison regiments and battalions, **noncombatant lower ranks** not holding noncommissioned officer ranks were given the **new pattern cap** [*shapka*] in place of the shako [*kiver*] and forage cap, identical to that established at this time for grenadier and musketeer regiments, except with the color red changed to yellow (Illus. 1787) (32).

20 February 1809 – The changes in the pattern and manner of wearing of the **knapsack** [*ranets*] introduced at this time for grenadier and musketeer regiments was extended with equal force to garrison regiments and battalions (Illus. 1787) (33).

4 April 1809 - **Noncommissioned officers** were ordered to have **galloon** not on the lower and side edges of the collar, but on the upper and side edges (34).

8 April 1809 – The changes in the manner of fitting **shoulder slings on muskets**, described in detail above for grenadier regiments, were also adopted in Garrisons (35).

20 April 1809 – The change in the manner of wearing the **knapsack**, introduced at this time for Army infantry, i.e. with the addition of a third belt over the chest, was also applied to garrison regiments and battalions [36].

8 June 1809 - The plumage around the sides of **generals' hats** was discontinued and the former pattern of buttonhole was replaced with a new one made of four thick twisted cords, of which the two middle ones are intertwined with each other as if in a plait [37].

13 October 1809 – The *Aland Garrison Regiment*, organized from the Kexholm, Novgorod, and Schlüsselburg battalions, was ordered to have the numeral 9 on its shoulder straps. The *Sveaborg Garrison Regiment*, formed from the Villmanstrand Battalion and a battalion of the Fredrikshamn Regiment was given the number 10, and the *Gangut Garrison Battalion*, renamed from the Pskov Battalion, was given the number 11 [37].

17 October 1809 – Lower ranks in garrison regiments and battalions were ordered to have **yellow buttons** instead of white on the **leggings** at the bottom of winter pants [39].

3 December 1809 – The tufts [*kisti*] above the shako pompons of lower combatant ranks in all garrison regiments and battalions were abolished, and the **pompons** [*repeiki*] themselves were prescribed to be of the following colors: *in the 1st battalion*—upper half green, lower half white; *in the 2nd*—upper half green, lower yellow; *in the 3rd*—upper half green, lower red; *in the 4th* and every separate battalion—all green [40].

In this same year the **powdering of the hair** was completely discontinued for officers, and for them as well as general officers it was permitted to wear double-breasted **frock coats** [*sertuki*] of dark-green cloth, with collars, cuffs, lining, and buttons in the same colors as on the tailcoat [41].

24 September 1810 - **Knapsack straps** were ordered to be stitched on the edges, in the manner of crossbelts and swordbelts, and have a bend at each shoulder [42]. In this same year the **plumes** on officers' hats were shortend [43].

29 April 1811 – Lower combatant ranks in the **Kazan Garrison Regiment** were ordered to have **grey coats** instead of dark-green, with the same turnbacks on the tails, red piping along the edges of the turnbacks, a white number on light-blue shoulder straps, and gray pants (Illus. 1788). Officers were given dark-green tailcoats and pants, the first with the same turnbacks on the tails and red piping along turnback edges (Illus. 1788), while the rest of the uniform and weaponry in this regiment remained as before [44]. These changes for the Kazan Regiment were a result of its inclusion into the newly established *Internal Guard* [*Vnutrennyaya Strazha*], into which were drawn all Garrisons except for the Moscow, Archangel, Orenburg, Tobolsk, Omsk, Irkutsk, Astrakhan, Kizlyar, Vladikavkaz, and Aktiar regiments, and the Arensburg, Kizilsk, Zverinogolovsk, Orel, Verkhneuralsk, newly formed Ural, Troitsk, Tomsk, Biisk, Petrovsk, Zhelezinsk, Semipalatinsk, Kamchatka, Baku, Derbent, and Mozdok battalions, as well as the further four battalions established in 1804 on the Orenburg Line. All these kept their previous uniforms, i.e. dark green with yellow collars and cuffs and a white number on red shoulder straps.

27 September 1811 – The battalions of the **Moscow Garrison Regiment** were ordered to have **shako pompons** in the following colors: 1st Battalion—white and green halves, 2nd—green and white halves, 3rd—dark-blue and white halves, 4th—green, 5th—green and dark-blue halves, and 6th—dark blue [45].

11 December 1811 – In place of the uniforms used by them since 1809, all lower **noncombatant ranks** in garrison units were given a new one identical to that established at this time for lower noncombatant ranks in grenadier and musketeer regiments, but with yellow piping (Illus. 1789) [46].

10 February 1812 – These same ranks in caftan coats and greatcoats were ordered to have **shoulder straps** of the same pattern and colors as the straps of combatant ranks [47], and about this same time there were the following changes in the uniforms of combatant ranks in garrison regiments and battalions:

1) New pattern **shako**, lower than before, with a greater spread or widening toward the top and indented sides, and now without sewn-on earflaps and neckflaps, these being henceforth worn separately (Illus. 1790).

2) High open **collars** were changed to low ones closed in front with small hooks (Illus. 1790).

3) Lower ranks' integral **leggings** [*kragi*] and officers' boots were to be high and up to the knees, the former having nine brass buttons (Illus. 1790).

4) Officers, in order to reduce their expenses, were permitted to have white **sashes** and **swordknots** [48].

31 December 1815 – All combatant ranks in garrison regiments and battalions, including the Kazan Regiment which had received the same uniform as other units, were ordered to have **red cuffs** on their coats (Illus. 1791), and **drummers' coats** were to be closed with small hooks and have sewn-on lace on both sides of the front opening (Illus. 1791). Beginning in this year, officers were required to wear a **cockade** on the hat that had a white ribbon around it, later changed to silver, and when in formation were to wear shakos with silver cords, pompon, chinscales, and the same cockade as on the hat (Illus. 1791) [49].

4 September 1816 – The two separate garrison battalions formed out of the Tobolsk Garrison Regiment were ordered to have numbers on their **shoulder straps**: *Tobolsk—24, Tomsk—18*, while the *Ust-Kamenogorsk Battalion* was given the number 33 [50]. In this same year **canes, non-commissioned officers' gloves, and halberds** were totally done away with, having since 1812 been gradually withdrawn from garrisons [51].

19 February 1818 – Garrison regiments and battalions were prescribed the following white numbers on red shoulder straps:

Arensburg Battalion – 1
Kazan Regiment – 2
Archangel Regiment – 3
Astrakhan Regiment – 4
Kizlyar Battalion – 5
Mozdok Battalion – 6
Vladikavkaz Regiment – 7
Orenburg Regiment – 8
Kizilsk Battalion – 9
Verkhneuralsk Battalion – 10
Troitsk Battalion – 11
Zverinogolovsk Battalion - 12
Orsk Battalion - 13
1st Orenburg Line Battalion – 14
2nd Orenburg Line Battalion – 15
3rd Orenburg Line Battalion – 16
4th Orenburg Line Battalion – 17
Tomsk Battalion – 18
Omsk Regiment – 19
Petrovsk Battalion – 20
Semipalatinsk Battalion – 21
Biisk Battalion – 22
Zhelezinsk Battalion – 23
Tobolsk Regiment – 24
Irkutsk Regiment – 25
Selenginsk Regiment – 26
Anapa Regiment – 27
Baku Battalion – 28
Derbent Battalion – 29
Guria Battalion – 30 [52].

In this same year **shakos** for garrison regiments and battalions began to be made higher than before, with flat tops instead of indented, as was laid down for army infantry regiments on 26 September 1817 [53].

5 February 1819 – Numbers on **shoulder straps**, instead of being thin worsted cord that was sewn on, were ordered to be cut out and backed from below with white cloth, and have a similarly constructed period or dot alongside the numeral [54].

23 December 1823 – The Archangel, Kazan, and Astrakhan Garrison Regiments, and the Arensburg, Tobolsk, Tomsk. and Irkutsk Garrison Battalions, having been included in the Separate Corps of the Internal Guard but serving detached from it, were ordered to have a white single-flame grenade on their **shakos** instead of a ribbon, and a white pompon with a red center (Illus. 1792) [55].

14 May 1821 – These same **shakos** were given to all garrison regiments and battalions of the Separate Caucasus Corps, Separate Orenburg Corps, and Separate Siberia Corps [56].

13 December 1824 – Lower combatant ranks of the Orenburg Garrison Regiment were ordered to have **shakos** with cords of the pattern used in the army infantry (Illus. 1793) [57].

15 December 1824 – The same kind of cords as well as white chinscales were ordered to be used in the **Archangel Garrison Regiment**. Along with this, **musicians** were introduced into that unit, not being authorized in any other garrisons. They received the same uniforms as musicians in infantry regiments except their swallows' nests were not in color of the shoulder straps, but dark green with red piping (Illus. 1794) [54].

29 March 1825 – For lower combatant ranks transferred to garrisons from the guards or army because of wounds or other debilities, there were established **chevrons** to be sewn onto the left sleeve to signify irreproachable service: for 10 years— one chevron, for 15 years—two, for 20 years—three, one above the other, all of yellow tape [59].

XVIII. BATTALIONS OF THE INTERNAL GUARD
[*Bataliony Vnutrennei Strazhi*]

29 April 1811 – With the establishment of the **Internal Guard** [*Vnutrenyaya Strazha*] all the battalions and half-battalions that were included in it were ordered to have the same uniform clothing as was prescribed on this same date for the Kazan Garrison Regiment and described in detail above. Since the Internal Guard as a whole was divided into districts [*okruga*], and districts into brigades, and brigades were made of battalions and half-battalions, each district was assigned its own number to be shown on shoulder straps and epaulettes. In each first brigade of a district the **shoulder straps and epaulettes** were red, in the second brigades—yellow, in the third—blue [*svetlosinii*], in the fourth—dark green with red pipin (Illus. 1795). In each first battalion or half-battalion in a brigade shako pompons were half white and half green; in each second battalion or half-battalion—half blue and and half white; in the third—half green and half blue (Illus. 1796). Officers of the first battalions or half-battalions in each brigade had dark-green flaps on thei coat cuffs; in the second battalions or half-battalions—dark green with yellow piping; in the third—yellow (Illus. 1797). On this basis, the distinctions between battalions and half-battalions of the Internal Guard were as follows [60]:

I District 1st Brigade:
Petrozavodsk Half-Battalion—red shoulder straps with No 1; pompons white and green; dark-green cuff flaps for officers. Kuopio Half-Battalion—red shoulder straps with No 1; pompons blue and white; officers' cuff flaps dark-green with yellow piping. Viborg Half-Battalion—red shoulder straps with No 1; pompons green and blue; yellow cuff flaps for officers.
I District 2nd Brigade:
St.-Petersburg Half-Battalion—yellow shoulder straps with No 1; pompons white and green; dark-green cuff flaps for officers. Novgorod Half-Battalion—yellow shoulder straps with No 1; pompons blue and white; officers' cuff flaps dark-green with yellow piping.
I District 3rd Brigade:
Reval Half-Battalion—blue shoulder straps with No 1; pompons white and green; dark-green cuff flaps for officers. Riga Half-Battalion—blue shoulder straps with No 1; pompons blue and white; officers' cuff flaps dark-green with yellow piping.
II District 1st Brigade:
Tver Half-Battalion—red shoulder straps with No 2; pompons white and green; dark-green cuff flaps for officers. Pskov Half-Battalion—red shoulder straps with No 2; pompons blue and white; officers' cuff flaps dark-green with yellow piping.
II District 2nd Brigade:
Vitebsk Half-Battalion—yellow shoulder straps with No 2; pompons white and green; dark-green cuff flaps for officers. Mitau Half-Battalion—yellow shoulder straps with No 2; pompons blue and white; officers' cuff flaps dark-green with yellow piping.
III District 1st Brigade:
Kaluga Half-Battalion—red shoulder straps with No 3; pompons white and green; dark-green cuff flaps for officers. Smolensk Half-Battalion—red shoulder straps with No 3; pompons blue and white; officers' cuff flaps dark-green with yellow piping. Mogilev Half-Battalion—red shoulder straps with No 3; pompons green and blue; yellow cuff flaps for officers.
III District 2nd Brigade:
Minsk Half-Battalion—yellow shoulder straps with No 3; pompons white and green; dark-green cuff flaps for officers. Vilna Half-Battalion—yellow shoulder straps with No 3; pompons blue and white; officers' cuff flaps dark-green with yellow piping.
IV District 1st Brigade:
Tula Half-Battalion—red shoulder straps with No 4; pompons white and green; dark-green cuff flaps for officers. Orel Half-Battalion—red shoulder straps with No 4; pompons blue and white; officers' cuff flaps dark-green with yellow piping. Chernigov Half-Battalion—red shoulder straps with No 4; pompons green and blue; yellow cuff flaps for officers.

IV District 2nd Brigade:

Grodno Half-Battalion—yellow shoulder straps with No 4; pompons white and green; dark-green cuff flaps for officers. Bialystok Half-Battalion—yellow shoulder straps with No 4; pompons blue and white; officers' cuff flaps dark-green with yellow piping.

V District 1st Brigade:

Kursk Half-Battalion—blue shoulder straps with No 5; pompons white and green; dark-green cuff flaps for officers. Kharkov Half-Battalion—blue shoulder straps with No 5; pompons blue and white; officers' cuff flaps dark-green with yellow piping. Poltava Half-Battalion—blue shoulder straps with No 5; pompons green and blue; yellow cuff flaps for officers. [The blue shoulder straps in this 1st Brigade are apparently a mistake by Viskovatov and should be red in order to maintain the pattern throughout the rest of this listing – M.C.]

V District 2nd Brigade:

Kiev Half-Battalion—yellow shoulder straps with No 5; pompons white and green; dark-green cuff flaps for officers. Zhitomir Half-Battalion—yellow shoulder straps with No 5; pompons blue and white; officers' cuff flaps dark-green with yellow piping.

VI District 1st Brigade:

Yekaterinoslav Half-Battalion—red shoulder straps with No 6; pompons white and green; dark-green cuff flaps for officers. Taurica Half-Battalion—red shoulder straps with No 6; pompons blue and white; officers' cuff flaps dark-green with yellow piping.Kherson Half-Batt.—red shoulder straps with No 6; pompons green and blue; yellow cuff flaps for officers.

VI District 2nd Brigade:

Kamenets-Podolsk Half-Battalion—yellow shoulder straps with No 6; pompons white and green; dark-green cuff flaps for officers. Tarnopol Half-Battalion—yellow shoulder straps with No 6; pompons blue and white; officers' cuff flaps dark-green with yellow piping.

VI District 1st Brigade:

Yekaterinoslav Half-Battalion—red shoulder straps with No 6; pompons white and green; dark-green cuff flaps for officers. Taurica Battalion—red shoulder straps with No 6; pompons blue and white; officers' cuff flaps dark-green with yellow piping. Kherson Battalion—red shoulder straps with No 6; pompons green and blue; yellow cuff flaps for officers.

VI District 2nd Brigade:

Kamenets-Podolsk Half-Battalion—yellow shoulder straps with No 6; pompons white and green; dark-green cuff flaps for officers. Tarnopol Half-Battalion—yellow shoulder straps with No 6; pompons blue and white; officers' cuff flaps dark-green with yellow piping.

VII District 1st Brigade:

Volgoda Half-Battalion—red shoulder straps with No 7; pompons white and green; dark-green cuff flaps for officers. Kostroma Half-Battalion—red shoulder straps with No 7; pompons blue and white; officers' cuff flaps dark-green with yellow piping.

VII District 2nd Brigade:

Vyatka Battalion—yellow shoulder straps with No 7; pompons white and green; dark-green cuff flaps for officers. Perm Half-Battalion—yellow shoulder straps with No 7; pompons blue and white; officers' cuff flaps dark-green with yellow piping.

VII District 3rd Brigade:

Kazan Garrison Regiment—blue shoulder straps with No 7; pompons white and green; dark-green cuff flaps for officers. Nizhnii-Novgorod Half-Battalion—blue shoulder straps with No 7; pompons blue and white; officers' cuff flaps dark-green with yellow piping.

VII District 4th Brigade:

Vladimir Half-Battalion—shoulder straps dark-green piped red, with No 7; pompons white and green; dark-green cuff flaps for officers. Yaroslavl Half-Battalion—shoulder straps dark-green piped red, with No 7; pompons blue and white; officers' cuff flaps dark-green with yellow piping.

VIII District 1st Brigade:

Ryazan Half-Battalion—red shoulder straps with No 8; pompons white and green; dark-green cuff flaps for officers. Tambov Half-Battalion—red shoulder straps with No 8; pompons blue and white; officers' cuff flaps dark-green with yellow piping. Penza Half-Battalion—red shoulder straps with No 8; pompons green and blue; yellow cuff flaps for officers.

VIII District 2nd Brigade:

Simbirsk Battalion—yellow shoulder straps with No 8; pompons white and green; dark-green cuff flaps for officers. Ufa Battalion—yellow shoulder straps with No 8; pompons blue and white; officers' cuff flaps dark-green with yellow piping.

VII District 3rd Brigade:
Saratov Half-Battalion—blue shoulder straps with No 8; pompons white and green; dark-green cuff flaps for officers. Voronezh Half-Battalion—blue shoulder straps with No 8; pompons blue and white; officers' cuff flaps dark-green with yellow piping.

3 July 1811 – Confirmation was given to a **table** of uniforms, accouterments, and weapons for battalions and half-battalions of the Internal Guard, based on which they kept the uniform clothing and armament described previously, with just the replacement of smooth black knapsacks with ones made from calf leather with the hair on the outside. Following the example of Garrison regiments and battalions, noncommissioned officers of the Internal Guard were prescribed gloves, canes, and halberds. Privates wore bayonets instead of short swords [61].

11 December 1811 – Lower **noncombatant** ranks of the Internal Guard were given new uniforms of the same pattern established on this date for noncombatant ranks in Garrison regiments and battalions, i.e. gray with yellow piping [62].

10 February 1812 – These same ranks in caftan coats and greatcoats were ordered to have **shoulder straps** of the same pattern and colors as the straps of combatant ranks [63], and about this same time there were the following changes in the uniforms of combatant ranks of the Internal Guard:

1) New pattern **shako**, lower than before, with a greater spread or widening toward the top and indented sides, and now without sewn-on earflaps and neckflaps, these being henceforth worn separately (Illus. 1798).

2) High open **collars** were changed to low ones closed in front with small hooks (Illus. 1798).

3) Lower ranks' integral **leggings** [*kragi*] and **officers' boots** were to be high and up to the knees, the former having nine brass buttons (Illus. 1798).

4) Officers, in order to reduce their expenses, were permitted to have white **sashes** and **swordknots** instead of silver [64].

31 December 1815 – **Drummers** in the Internal Guard were ordered to have new coats closed with small hooks and have sewn-on lace on both sides of the front opening (Illus. 1799). Beginning in this year, officers started to wear a **cockade** on the hat that had a white ribbon around it, later changed to silver [65].

21 May 1816 – Field and company-grade officers of Internal Guard battalions were permitted to wear gray cloth **riding trousers** with yellow piping and stripes (called *lampasy*) (Illus. 1800) [66].

10 September 1816 – Non-commissioned officers' **halberds** were withdrawn, and they were ordered to have muskets and pouches when in formation. These last items were of the same pattern as confirmed on 26 September 1817 for Army infantry, but without badges [67].

18 May 1817 – Confirmation was given to a new **table** of uniform clothing, accouterments, and arms, in which the gloves and canes still retained by Internal Guard non-commissioned officers were withdrawn, and the 26 September 1817 rules for constructing shakos and other accouterments were adopted, as for Army infantry regiments (Illus. 1801). Along with this the former pattern of **forage cap** with tassels was replaced one that was round and made of gray cloth with a yellow band. On **shoulder straps** the sewn-on numbers were replaced by cut-outs backed by yellow cloth for red, blue, and dark-green straps, and by red cloth for yellow straps [68].

20 February 1818 – In accordance with a newly compiled listing of Internal Guard battalions, they were ordered to have the following **shoulder straps**:

I District: 1st Brigade – Mitau and Riga – red.
    2nd Brigade: Reval and Pskov – yellow.
II District: 1st Brigade – Vitebsk and Smolensk – red.
    2nd Brigade: Mogilev and Kaluga – yellow.
III District: 1st Brigade – Chernigov and Kiev – red.
    2nd Brigade: Poltava, Kharkov, and Kursk – yellow.
IV District: 1st Brigade – Kishinev and Kherson – red.
    2nd Brigade: Yekaterinoslav and Taurica – yellow.
V District: 1st Brigade – Viborg and Kuopio – red.
    3rd Brigade: Petrozavodsk and Vologda – blue (Note: The 2nd Brigade consisted of the Archangel Garrison Reg which belonged to the Corps of the Internal Guard only for unit listings, but not in matters of uniform.)

VI District: 1st Brigade – St. Petersburg and Novgorod – red.
    2nd Brigade: Tver and Yaroslavl – yellow.
    3rd Brigade: Vladimir and Kostroma – blue.
VII District: 1st Brigade – Moscow and Ryazan – red.
    2nd Brigade: Tula and Orel – yellow.
    3rd Brigade: Voronezh and Tambov – blue.
VIII District: 1st Brigade – Vyatka, Perm, and Ufa – red (Note: This District comprised only one brigade.)
IX District: 1st Brigade – Nizhnii-Novgorod and Simbirsk – red.
    2nd Brigade: Saratov and Penza – yellow.
X District: 1st Brigade – Georgievsk and Tiflis – red.
XI District: 1st Brigade – Tobolsk, Tomsk, and Irkutsk – red.
XII District: 1st Brigade – Vilna and Minsk – red.
    2nd Brigade: Grodno and Bialystok – yellow.
    3rd Brigade: Zhitomir and Kamenets-Podolsk – blue.

The numbers on the **shoulder straps** corresponded to the district number, and in all else the distinctions between battalions remained the same as laid down on 29 April 1811 [69].

2 May 1822 – Instead of dark-green **pants**, company-grade officers of the Internal Guard were ordered to wear in winter the riding trousers established in 1816, and in summer—linen pants with integral spats [*kozyrki*], Both of these would be worn with **shakos**—hats were abolished. Field-grade officers when with the troops [*dlya fronta*], for both winter and summer, were left with dark-green pants and high boots with spurs (Illus. 1802) [70].

23 December 1823 – The Internal Guard was ordered to have **shakos** with a white single-flame grenade in place of the ribbon or cockade used up to this time (Illus. 1803) [71].

29 March 1825 - For lower combatant ranks transferred to the Internal Guard from the Guards or Army because of wounds or other debilities, there were established **chevrons** of yellow tape to signify irreproachable service, of the same appearance and in accordance with the same rules as described above for garrison regiments and battalions [72].

XIX. GENDARMES OF THE INTERNAL GUARD
[*Zhendarmy Vnutrennei Strazhi*]

18 May 1817 – Confirmation was given to a **table** of uniform clothing, accouterments, and arms for these units included in the Internal Guard: the *Gendarme Battalions [Zhandarmskie diviziony]* in the two capital cities; *Gendarme commands* in provincial capitals and port towns; and the *Gendarme command* in the town of Tsarskoe Selo. Based on this table and on special HIGHEST Orders from 1 February through 15 May of this year, they were prescribed to have [73]:

a) *Gendarme battalions:*
Privates – all uniform clothing, weapons, and horse furniture were as established on 30 August 1815 and 15 May 1817 for privates of the Gendarme Regiment, described above under Army cavalry, but without aiguilettes, with yellow piping and yellow riding-trouser stripes instead of red, and with white monograms and crowns on the horse cloths instead of red, these being edged with thin yellow cord (Illus. 1804).
Non-commissioned officers – The same as privates but with the distinctions as in the Gendarme Regiment, set forth above in the description of their uniform (Illus. 1805).
Trumpeters – Also as for privates and with the same distinctions as in the Gendarme Regiment (Illus. 1806).
Officers – The same as in the Gendarme Regiment but without aiguilettes and buttonhole loops on the coat, and red changed to yellow throughout (Illus. 1807).

b) *Provincial and Port Gendarme commands:*
Privates and non-commissioned officers – In all respects as for privates and non-commissioned officers of Gendarme battalions, except with yellow cloth shoulder straps instead of epaulettes (Illus. 1808 and 1809).
Officers – In all respects as for officers of Gendarme battalions.

c) *Tsarskoe-Selo Gendarme Command:*
Privates and non-commissioned officers – In all respects as for these ranks in the Gendarme battalions.

29 March 1825 – For lower ranks in Gendarme battalions and commands there was established sewn-on **chevrons** of yellow tape to denote irreproachable service, identical in form and following the same rules as described above for Garrison regiments and battalions [74].

XX. INVALID COMPANIES AND COMMANDS
Established Before the Formation of the Internal Guard and Mobile Invalid Companies in 1811.

[*Invalidnyya roty i komandy, uchrezhdennyya do obrazovaniya v 1811 godu vnutrennei strazhi i podvizhnykh invalidnykh rot.*]

9 April 1801 – Lower ranks in invalid companies and commands were ordered to cut off their **curls** and have **queues** only 4 vershoks [7 inches] long, tying them midway down the collar [75].

30 April 1802 - Confirmation was given to a new **table of uniforms, accouterments, and weapons** for the invalid companies that were authorized as one in each Garrison battalion on the internal establishment. Based on this table the following was prescribed:

Invalid privates – coat of older or newer style [*kaftan ili mundir*], pants, neckcloth, boots, greatcoat, forage cap, and hat, the same as in Garrison regiments except that the last item had no ribbon or cockade and only a button. Also, a sword [*shpaga*] with a short-sword blade [*tesachnyi klinok*] and white sword knot, and a sword belt around the waist (Illus. 1810).

Invalid drummers – the same as for privates, with the usual distinctions as in Army infantry and Garrisons (Illus. 1812).

Barbers and *lazaret orderlies* – the same as these ranks in Garrisons.

Knapsacks and water flasks were not prescribed for invalids [76].

Invalid company-grade officers – uniforms as for garrison company-grade officers, but without spontoons (Illus. 1813) [77]. Invalid companies were differentiated between themselves by the colors for collars, cuffs, and shoulder straps, which were the same for them as for the battalions to which they belonged [78].

20 August 1806 – For invalids as part of Garrisons as well as in independent units, there were established dark-green **coats** with likewise dark-green collars, cuffs, and coattail lining and turnbacks, and with white buttons: four along the front openning and one below, under the sword belt; dark-green—white in summertime—linen pants; army infantry shako with a small worsted tassel the same color as the shoulder straps (Illus. 1814). For invalids in garrison regiments and battalions had **shoulder straps** of the same color as the regimental or battalion straps. For invalids at the Alexander Manufactory, these were red; at the Gatchina Palace—white; at the Pavlovsk Palace—yellow [79].

2 December 1806 – Lower ranks of invalid companies and commands were ordered to cut their **hair** short; officers, however, were in this case allowed to proceed according to their personal inclination [80].

23 December 1807 – Invalid companies which were part of a Garrison were given new patterns of **winter pants** with integral leggings and white buttons (Illlus. 1815), and of **summer pants** with integral spats as established at this same time for Army infantry and Garrisons (Illus. 1816) [81].

2 November 1808 – The aforementioned **pants** were kept only for privates, non-commissioned officers, and drummers, while barbers and lazaret orderlies were ordered to have pants as well as boots of the patterns established in 1802 [82].

17 October 1809 – It was ordered to have iron buttons on the integral **leggings** of winter pants instead of white [83].

XXI. MOBILE INVALID COMPANIES.
[*Podvizhnyya invalidnyya roty*]

27 March and **3 July 1811** – With the division of all invalids as mobile, serving, and non-serving, and the formation of the first *Mobile invalid companies*, these lower ranks were prescribed the same **uniforms** and **arms** as received at this time by battalions and half-battalions of the Internal Guard, except coats and greatcoats were all gray. The first had four buttons alongside the front openning, gray shoulder straps with a yellow company number, dark-green shako pompons, and black sword belts, crossbelts, musket slings, and lock covers (Illus. 1817 and 1818). Officers were given completely dark-green uniforms, silver epaulettes with the likewise silver company number on a dark-green cloth field, and hats with a silver buttonhole loop and black plume (Illus. 1819) [84].

31 December 1815 – Lower ranks of Mobile invalid companies were ordered to have **dark-green coats** instead of gray, with six buttons on each side of the front, and a collar closed with small hooks (Illus. 1820) [85]. In this same year officers of these companies began to wear on their hats a cockade with white ribbon around it (Illus. 1820), later changed to silver [86].

20 February 1816 – For lower ranks gray **pants** were changed to dark green (Illus. 1820) [87].

1 September 1816 – It was ordered that these ranks have **shakos** and **summer pants** of the same patterns as in use at this time in Internal Guard battalions [88].

8 October 1817 – These same ranks were ordered to have **shakos**, **summer pants**, and **integral leggings** of the patterns pre-scribed for Internal Guard battalions, based on the HIGHEST confirmed table for them of 18 May 1817 (Illus. 1821) [89].

5 February 1819 – Reserve Mobile invalid companies were given **knapsacks** and **canteens**, or water flasks [*manerki, ili vodnosnyya flyazhki*] (Illus. 1822) [90].

14 May 1824 – The ribbon or cockade on **shakos** in Mobile invalid companies was replaced by a white grenade with a single flame (Illus. 1823) [91].

29 March 1825 - For lower ranks transferred to Mobile invalid companies from the Guards or Army because of wounds or other debilities, there were established **chevrons** of yellow tape to signify irreproachable service, identical to and worn according to the same rules as for those described above for garrison regiments and battalions [92].

XXII. DISTRICT INVALID COMMANDS.

[*Uezdnya invalidnyya komandy*]

27 March and 3 July 1811 – Privates, non-commissioned officers, and drummers in *Serving district invalid commands* [*Sluzhashchiya uezdnyya invalidnyya komandy*] received the exact same uniform clothing as established at this time for Mobile invalid companies, but without muskets and pouches, and instead of shakos they had round forage caps of gray cloth with a leather visor (Illus. 1824). Officers were given the same uniforms as officers of the above referenced Mobile companies [93].

23 and 31 December 1815 – Officers and lower ranks of *Serving district invalid commands* were ordered to have yellow coat **cuffs**, with the first of these having the fields of their **epaulettes** and the second their **shoulder straps**—of the same colors as the epaulettes and shoulder straps in those garrison regiments and battalions to which the commands belonged (Illus. 1825). Lower ranks in *non-serving commands* were prescribed the same **shoulder straps** as for serving, while cuffs were of the previous color, i.e. gray. Along with this, serving as well as non-serving invalids were prescribed to have six **buttons** along each side of the coat's front opening instead of four, and **collars** were to be closed with small hooks (Illus. 1825) [94]. In this same year officers began to wear **cockades** on their hats, with white ribbon around them, later changed to silver [95].

21 May 1816 – Field and company-grade officers of district invalid commands were allowed to wear gray cloth riding trousers with yellow stripes and piping [96].

9 June 1817 – Serving invalid companies were ordered to be equipped with muskets with bayonets [97].

8 October 1817 – Serving and non-serving invalids were ordered to have **shakos**, **summer pants**, and **integral leggings** of the patterns prescribed for Internal Guard battalions, based on the HIGHEST confirmed table for them of 18 May 1817 (Illus. 1826) [98].

25 October 1817 – Lower ranks privided with muskets in serving invalid commands were ordere to have their **short swords** withdrawn [99].

9 February 1822 – Instead of hats, which were withdrawn, field and company-grade officers in commands of non-serving invalids were ordered to wear **shakos** identical to those in use at this time by officers of the Internal Guard (Illus. 1827), and in place of silver sashes they were to have one of thread [*nityanye*] [100].

2 May 1822 – Company-grade officers of district invalid commands were ordere to wear gray **riding trousers** with yellow stripes and piping in winter instead of dark-green pants, and in summer—white linen pants with spats. Both pants and trousers were to be worn with **shakos** of the same pattern as used at this time by officers in Internal Guard battalions [101].

14 May 1824 – The ribbon or cockade on **shakos** in district invalid commands was replaced by a grenade with a single flame (Illus. 1828) [102].

29 March 1825 - For lower ranks transferred to district invalid commands from the Guards or Army because of wounds or other debilities, there were established **chevrons** of yellow tape to signify irreproachable service, identical to and worn according to the same rules as for those described above for garrison regiments and battalions [103].

XXIII. ÉTAPE INVALID COMMANDS

[*Etapnyya invalidnyya komandy*]

These commands, first established on 9 May 1817, had the same **uniforms** and **arms** throughout as had been prescribed for district commands of serving invalids [104], and those which escorted arrested persons along the road to Siberia were by a HIGHEST Order of 21 February 1820 supplied with additional **warm clothing**, viz.: warm caps with ear flaps or covers, short fur coats [*polushubki*], felt boots [*valenyya sapogi*] reaching above the knee and lined with leather, socks and sole inserts, and warm pants worn over the boots, of gray cloth [105].

XXIV. SALT INVALID COMMANDS

[*Solyanyya invalidnyya komandy*]

The **Crimea Salt Command** [*Krymskaya Solyanaya komanda*], established at the Crimean Saltworks in 1805, was uniformed before 23 April 1819 (when it was assigned to the Taurica Internal Garrison Battalion) on the basis of the Highest Ukase of 20 August 1806 referenced above in Chapter XX. From 1819 its **uniform**, as well as that of Salt commands established on 5 August 1818: *Kamyshinsk, Astrakhan, Mozharsk, Staraya-Russa, Dedyukhin, Onega,* and *Ledenga*—followed the patterns used by serving invalids [106].

XXV. SETTLED INVALIDS

[*Poselennye invalidy*]

15 November 1816 – When *serving* and *non-serving invalid commands* were established for settled regiments they were prescribed the following **uniform**: dark-green coat with similarly colored collar and cuffs and red lining on the skirts and turnbacks, shoulder straps of the same color as for the regiment to which the command belonged, and with white buttons; dark-green pants; gray greatcoat with dark-green collar; the same shako as the regiment's combatant ranks but with white fittings, white pompon with a red center; white sword belt. Invalids in regiments that had shakos with badges for distinction were likewise authorized these badges (Illus. 1829). This regulation applied to both infantry and cavalry [107].

2 November 1817 – Supplementary to this order, *invalids of settled cavalry regiments* were directed to have the same **shako** as in the infantry [108].

19 July 1818 – Supplementary to the two preceding orders, *serving invalids in settled regiments* were directed to have dark-green **shoulder straps** and infantry **short swords**, and those in Lancer regiments were to wear a **shako** with a white single-flame grenade (Illus. 1830). *Non-serving invalids* were prescribed the exact same uniform but the coat had dark-green lining on the skirts and turnbacks and the shako had no cords (Illus. 1831) [109].

5 November 1823 – Invalids of settled cavalry regiments were ordered to have the same **uniform** as Mobile invalids [110].

XXVI. MILITARY ORPHANS' DETACHMENTS AND MILITARY CANTONIST DETACHMENTS

[*Voenno-sirotskiya otdeleniya i otdeleniya voennykh kantonistov*]

9 April 1801 - Lower ranks in *Military Orphans' Detachments* were ordered to cut off their **curls** and have **queues** only 4 vershoks [7 inches] long, tying them midway down the collar [111].

2 December 1806 – Lower ranks in *Military Orphans' Detachments* were ordered to cut their **hair** short [112].

25 September 1809 – Non-commissioned officers and teachers (from lower ranks) in these Detachments were ordered to have the same **uniforms** as established for invalids on 20 August 1806 [113].

10 March 1816 – It was permitted that **greatcoats** be made for pupils in Military Orphans' Detachments in the Southern region instead of fur coats [*shuby*] [114].

15 November 1816 – With the establishment of *Military Cantonist Detachments* among the settled troops, these were prescribed the following **uniform**: jacket of dark-green cloth, of the pattern used by naval équipages, with normal infantry cuff flaps of the same cloth; red collar and cuffs; shoulder straps of the same color as for the regiment to which the Detachment belonged, with brass buttons; winter pants or *sharavary* of dark-green cloth, but in summer of linen, both kinds being of the naval pattern; dark-green forage caps with the same colored cap band, red piping, leather visor, and a chin strap fastened below by a button (Illus. 1832) [115].

4 August 1817 – Pupils of the St.-Peterburg Military Orphans' Detachment were prescribed the same pattern of **uniform** as described in the preceding paragraph, but the jacket and cuff flaps were gray; collar, cuffs, and shoulder straps yellow, buttons white, winter pants gray, forage caps gray with a yellow band, without visors (Illus. 1833) [116].

15 August 1817 – This **uniform** was extended to the other Military Orphans' Detachments [117].

2 November 1817 – Military cantonists with Settled Lancer regiments were ordered to be uniformed in the pattern established 15 November 1816, but the clothing was to be of **dark-blue** cloth instead of dark green, and collar, cuffs, shoulder straps, and buttons were the regimental colors (Illus. 1834) [118].

30 December 1818 – It was ordered to supply older cantonists [*bol'shago vozrasta kantonisty*] in the Military Settlements with **greatcoats** at government expense [119].

16 June 1819 – Cantonists in the Military Settlements were ordered to button the chinstrap of their **forage caps** only when in formation [*vo fronte*], and the rest of the time they were to tuck the strap inside the cap. At the bottom of their **pants** they were to have leather straps called *pomochi* under the boots [120].

5 July 1821 – Military Cantonists in the Instructional squadrons and battalions of Settled Lancer and Infantry regiments were ordered to have: the first—**lancer headdresses**, and the second—**infantry shakos**. Both were to be in black oilcloth covers. Cantonists throughout the Settled Cavalry were to wear single-breasted **jackets** with nine buttons and gray **riding trousers** with stripes instead of pants, of the pattern prescribed for combatant lower ranks (Illus. 1835) [121].

21 October 1821 – These cantonists were ordered to have **forage caps** without visors [122].

XXVII. PROVINCIAL COMPANIES and STATE COMMANDS
[*Gubernskiya roty i shtatnyya komandy*]

9 April 1801 – Lower ranks of *provincial companies* (found in provincial and territorial capitals) and *state commands* (in district seats), which before 1811 performed the functions of the Internal Guard, were ordered to Lower ranks in *Military Orphans' Detachments* were ordered to cut off their **curls** and have **queues** only 4 vershoks [7 inches] long, tying them midway down the collar [123].

20 October 1806 – Lower ranks of these companies and commands were ordered to cut off their queues and keep their hair short, while in matter officers were allowed to proceed according to their own desire Lower ranks in *Military Orphans' Detachments* were ordered to cut off their **curls** and have **queues** only 4 vershoks [7 inches] long, tying them midway down the collar [124]. Along with this it was allowed to issue arms to these ranks as follows: instead of musketeer firearms—jäger firearms, as well as cavalry carbines and *shtutser* rifles, and instead of short swords—sabers, broad swords, and bayonets without distinction, provided only that they be fit for use [125]. In regard to uniforms, before 1807 there were no directives and their appearance remained the same as in the preceding reign.

2 August 1807 – These companies and commands were forbidden to wear **coats** of the pattern used at this time in the Army, but were ordered to have them of the previous pattern but with a standing collar, with six buttons, single breasted as for the army; pants of gray cloth, lined at the bottom with leather and six buttons the same color as the coat buttons. Along with this it was allowed to wear musketeer shakos, but also to have the three-cornered hats introduced in 1801 (Illus. 1836) [126]. With this uniform, the privates, non-commissioned officers, drummers, and field-grade officers in foot units, as well as dragoons in provincial and territorial companies all had collars, cuffs, and buttons according to the colors prescribed for the province [*guberniya*] [127].

4 August 1808 – In response to the Army's need for cloth, in all provinces the uniforms for provincial companies and state commands that were made from such material were ordered to be made from peasant cloth [*krest'yanskoe sukno*], but for collars and cuffs colored cloth would be used, according to provincial distinctions (Illus. 1837) [128].

3 August 1809 – Confirmation was given to a listing of colors for provincial **uniform coats**, based on which the collars, cuffs, and buttons for provincial companies and state commands were as follows:

a) Provinces of the 1st Group [*1-go razbora*].
St.-Petersburg, Lifland, Nizhnii-Novgorod, Moscow, Kostroma, Tula, and Vilna—red collar and cuffs, yellow buttons; Tver, Vologoda, Vladimir, Perm, Finland, and Grodno—red collar and cuffs, white buttons (Illus. 1837).
b) Provinces of the 2nd Group.
Voronezh, Orel, Kursk, Tobolsk, and Kiev—sky-blue collar and cuffs, yellow buttons; Saratov, Kaluga, Pskov, Tambov, Astrakhan, Simbirsk, and Courland—sky-blue collar and cuffs, white buttons (Illus. 1837).
c) Provinces of the 3rd Group.
Penza and Tomsk—dark-green collar and cuffs, yellow buttons; Irkutsk, Archangel, and Olonets—dark-green collar and cuffs, white buttons (Illus. 1838). Poltava—light-green collar and cuffs, yellow buttons; Slobodsko-Ukraine and Chernigov—light-green collar and cuffs, white buttons (Illus. 1838).
d) Provinces of the 4th Group.
Kherson, Taurica, and Minsk—black collar and cuffs, yellow buttons; Yekaterinoslav, Bialystok, and Vyatka—black collar

and cuffs, white buttons (Illus. 1838).

e) Provinces of the 5th Group.

Vitebsk—very dark blue collar and cuffs, yellow buttons; Caucaus, Estonia, and Mogilev— very dark blue collar and cuffs, white buttons (Illus. 1839).

f) Provinces of the 6th Group.

Georgia—violet collar and cuffs, white buttons (Illus. 1839).

g) Provinces of the 7th Group.

Smolensk—raspberry collar and cuffs, white buttons (Illus. 1840).

h) Provinces of the 8yh Group.

Ryazan, Podolia, Volhynia, Novgorod, and Yaroslavl—orange collar and cuffs, yellow buttons; Kazan and Orenburg—orange collar and cuffs, white buttons (Illus. 1840) [129].

XXVIII. MINES BATTALIONS.

[*Gornye bataliony*]

8 July 1820 – *Mines battalions Nos. 1, 2, 3, 4,and* 5, formed from various commands at mining works, were given blue [*svetlosinii*] single-breasted coats with yellow piping on the collar, cuffs, cuff flaps, down the front opening to the skirts, and on the skirt turnbacks, with white buttons; garrison shako of the pattern in use at that time, with a cockade in front and a white over green pompon; blue pants with integral leather leggings fastened with nine brass buttons. Other items of uniform clothing, as well as all accouterments and weapons, remained as before, i.e. the same as prescribed for garrison regiments and battalions. Battalions were distinguished by their number: for lower ranks in blue on yellow shoulder straps with blue piping, and for officers—in silver on the yellow field of the epaulettes (Illus. 1841 and 1842) [130].

XXIX. RECRUITS.

[*Rekruty*]

Before 23 May 1808 recruits were accepted from their landowner donors wearing normal peasant caftan tunics [*kaftany*], breeches of coarse peasant cloth [*sermyazhnye shtany*], and peasant shoes [*chiriki*] or boots [*upaki*] [131]. [Although the word "recruit" was used, men for the army were not voluntarily recruited, but compulsorily conscripted – M.C.]

23 May 1808 – So that recruits would have clothing suitable for service at the very start of their acceptance into the army, it was ordered that there be made for them **gray cloth caftans or tailcoats** [*kaftany ili mundiry*] of soldier pattern with covered buttons; pants and forage caps of plain peasant cloth; black neckcloths; peasant boots either smeared with clean tar [*chistym degtem vymazannye*] or made with the hair side of the leather on the outside [*lichnye sapogi*]; gray cloth pouches to substitute for knapsacks and hold any baggage. (Illus. 1843); and peasant shirts and winter coats [*shuby*] as before. Of these items the caftan coat, pants, neckcloth, and so-called knapsacks were made by the government and charged to the recruits' donors, while the rest, as well as underclothing and winter and summer foot cloths [*podvertki*] were provided by the donors in kind [132].

28 July 1809 – It was emphasized that recruits were to be received from their donors with new **winter coats** [*shuby*] without exception, and not half-coats [*polushubki*] [133].

27 June 1812 – The **forage caps** with hanging tassel prescribed for recruits was replaced by low caps without tassels, of the pattern used as this time in the Army (Illus. 1844) [134].

8 July 1812 – The cloth, linen, and other items stipulated for recruit **clothing** were ordered to be given by the donors in kind [135].

8 June 1816 – The items levied from donors in kind were replaced by a **monetary payment** to the treasury, and subsequently recruits were clothed at Internal Guard battalions: in each province—two-thirds of recruits in infantry uniforms, and one-third in the clothing for jägers regiments. This **uniform clothing** was to consist of a forage cap with band but without the piping used to distinguish companies within regiments, greatcoats and tailcoats without shoulder straps but with the full number of buttons, winter pants with integral leggings and buttons, neckcloth with dicky, boots, gloves, and a cloth knapsack (Illus. 1845) [136].

Russian Officer 1814

XXX. MILITARY ADMINISTRATION OFFICIALS NOT BELONGING TO TROOP UNITS.

[Chiny voennago vedomstva, v sostave voisk nevoshedshie]

a) *Officials of the Government Military Collegium and its Executive Offices.*

23 March 1801 – Field and company-grade officers of the Military Collegium and its Executive Offices [*Voennaya Kollegiya i eya Ekspeditsii*], wearing the uniforms specified for them in the preceding reign, were ordered to have sword knots on their swords [137].

30 January 1802 – Officer ranks on official Commissariat and Provisioning establishment tables were ordered to wear the common army uniform [138]. (Note: This uniform will be described later in the section for general officers, adjutants, and other military officials.)

17 March 1802 – Chancellery employees [*kantselyarskie sluzhiteli*]of the Military College and its Executive Offices were ordered to wear dark-green cloth tailcoats of the same cut and with the same number of gilt buttons as in the Army, with collar, slit cuffs, and turnback skirts of dark-green cloth,; red cloth piping on the edged of the collar and cuffs and along the skirt turnbacks; and dark-green stamin lining. A white cloth waistcoat was prescribed with this coat. Pants were either deerskin [*losinnyi*] or cloth, boots with blunt toes and reaching one vershok [1-3/4 inches] below the knee, black silk neckcloth, hat of the same size and pattern as established at this time for infantry officers but without any fittings apart from a cord for tying it up and a ribbon or cockade with a button, officer-pattern greatcoat—of gray with dark-green cloth lining, sword of the pattern for infantry officers but without a sword knot (Illus. 1846). Personnel holding field or company-grade officer rank were prescribed boots with iron spurs, the exact same hats as for infantry officers, with buttonhole loop and plume, and swords with sword knots (Illus. 1847) [139].

19 June 1806 – Comptrolers in the Military Collegium's Accounting Office [*Kontrolery Voennoi Kollegii Schetnoi Ekspeditsii*] were ordered to wear the common army uniform, while Secretaries and chancellery officials were to wear the Military Collegium uniform as before, but with white buttons [140].

21 June 1806 – Officials in the Military Collegium who wear the Military-Collegium uniform were ordered to wear hats without plumes [140].

1 February 1808 – New uniforms were established for officials of the Military Collegium and its Executive Offices except for the Commissariat and Provisioning Office. The uniforms were divided into four categories [*razryady*]:

1st Category, general officers – for all officials of the Collegium and its Executive Offices—a dark-green tailcoat, single breasted, with red piping on the collar, cuffs (slit), and skirt turnbacks, with gold buttons, dark-green lining, and gold embroidery on the collar and cuffs consisting of a narrow gold border along the edges, tracery along the border in the form of S-shapes [*zmeiki*, literally "serpants"] and leaves, and two wavy buttonhole loops (Illus. 1848). Pants remained white; boots had spurs; hats were as for infantry officers, with white plumage around the brim; and the sword was as for infantry officers, with a swordknot (Illus. 1849).

2nd Category, field-grade officiers – for Military Councilors, Comptrollers, and persons authorized to attend meetings in the Executive Offices [*Voennye Sovetniki, Kontrolery i prisutstvuyushchie v Ekspeditsiyakh*]—similar to the the preceding, but without embroidered tracery between the border and buttonhole loops, and hats without plumage (Illus. 1850 and 1851).

3rd Category, field-grade officiers – for Senior Secretaries [*Ober-Sekretari*] and other officials in the Military Collegium—also similar to the preceding but with a single buttonhole loop on the collar and cuffs, no gold border, and hats without plumage (Illus. 1852).

4th Category, company-grade officers – for the same officials as above—similar to the preceding but without any embroidery (Illus. 1852).

The uniform of the 3rd category was specifically for distinguished and zealous service, awarded upon review by the Minister of War and confirmed by the Military Collegium. Unitl they received it, officials had to wear the uniform of the 4th category [142].

13 February 1808 – It was decided by the Minister of Military Land Forces that from from 13 February of this year Commissioners whose assignment to the Commissariat and Provisioning establishments he himself confirmed would be prescribed to wear the military-collegium uniform of the 4th category, allowing, however, those who displayed distinction in carrying out of their duties and making efficient use of government funds to wear the 3rd-category uniform [143].

8 March 1808 – Military Collegium officials with the right to wear the 2nd-category uniform and holding 5th-class rank were ordered to wear hats with plumage in the manner of general officers [144].

3 March 1809 – Chancellery employees of the Military Collegium and its Executive Offices along with their subordinate branches were, in place of tailcoats [*mundiry*], given single-breasted uniform frock coats [*sertuki*], keeping, however, the colors that were prescribed for the tailcoat, i.e. entirely dark green with red piping, yellow buttons, and dark-green stamin lining (Illus. 1853) [145].

8 July 1809 – The plumage on the hats of Military-Collegium officials of 5th class and higher was abolished and the former pattern of buttonhole loop replaced by a new one consisting of four thick bullion cords of which the two middle ones were braided together in the form of a plait (Illus. 1854). Around this time all Military-Collegium officials were allowed to wear dark-green pants for everyday wear instead of white. They were also given dark-green frock coats with the same buttons and collar as on the tailcoat, but without embroidery [146].

b) Officials in the Department of Land Forces

25 March 1803 – Officials who had come to the Department of Land Forces [*Departament voenno-sukhoputnykh sil*] from both military or civil service were ordered to wear the uniform established for the Military Collegium unless they had received personal permission to wear army uniforms [147].

c) Officials of the War Ministry.

27 January 1812 – With the reorganization of the Government Military Collegium into the War Ministry [*Voennoe Ministerstvo*], all its classed officials were ordered to wear the uniform defined on 1 February 1808 for officials, and chancellery employees—that of 3 March 1809 for Collegium chancellery employees. The only difference was that beginning in this year collars began to be lower than before and closed by small hooks (Illus. 1855) [148].

In 1814 – Officials in the War Ministry were ordered to wear hats with white tape around the cockade, later changed to silver [149].

11 March 1816 – All classed officials of the Artillery and Engineer Departments of the War Ministry were ordered to wear the current uniforms prescribed for the Ministry, but those in the personal Chancelleries of the Inspectors of Artillery and Engineers were to have a uniform of the pattern confirmed on 12 February of the this year for officials on His Imperial Majesty's Main Staff, as described below [150].

27 November 1816 – New uniform clothing was established for guards [*vakhtery*] of the War Ministry's Commissariat and Provisioning Departments: dark-green coat, single-breasted with nine buttons, the same color for shoulder straps, collar, slit cuffs, turnbacks and skirt lining, brass buttons; dark-green pants with short integral leggings closed by seven brass buttons; gray greatcoat with dark-green collar and shoulder straps, brass buttons; infantry pattern shako without chinscales, with a dark-green pompon and a ribbon or cockade (of black tape with orange edges) instead of a coat-of-arms plate; dark-green forage cap and an infantry short sword worn on a black sword belt (Illus. 1856). Personnel in non-commissioned officers' ranks were distinguished by gold galloon on the coat's collar and cuffs and a non-commissioned officer's pompon on the shako [151].

29 May 1817 – *Guards and employees* [*vakhtery i sluzhiteli*] of the above two Departments were ordered to be differentiated by letters on the shoulder straps, made from thin yellow cord: in the Commissariat Department—Cyrillic *K*., in the Provisioning—Cyrillic *P*. [appearing to Western eyes as the Greek letter pi] [152].

d) Officials under the General Staff before it became part of His Imperial Majesty's Main Staff.

9 August 1811 – *Lower ranks* assigned to the *General Staff building* [*Dom General'nago Shtaba*] were given uniforms as follows: dark-green single-breasted frock coat [*sertuk*] with black shoulder straps, collar, and cuffs, with red piping on the collar, cuffs, and skirt turnbacks (these last being lined in red), brass buttons; dark-green pants with leather reinforcements or leggings, but in summer white pants of Flemish linen; gray greatcoat with the same colors for shoulder straps, collar, and cuffs as on the frock coat; round dark-green forage cap with a black visor and red piping (Illus. 1857). Non-commissioned officers had gold galloon on the collar and cuffs [153].

23 January 1812 – *Government master craftsmen* [*kazennye masterovye*] in the *machine workshop* [*mekhanicheskaya masterskaya*] established under the General Staff were prescribed the exact same uniform as given on 17 December 1811 to non-combatants in the Artillery, but with the addition of red shoulder straps (Illus. 1858) [154].

e) Officials of His Imperial Majesty's Main Staff.

12 February 1816 – *Classed officials of His Imperial Majesty's Main Staff* were ordered to have the uniform given to these same ranks in the War Ministry, but the tailcoat's cuffs were not slit but round, with red piping and red cloth cuff flaps, and on the flaps three gold embroidered buttonhole loops for those personnel who had these prescribed for their collars (Illus. 1859). Clerks [pisarya] were given dark-green frock coats [sertuki] with likewise dark-green collar and cuffs, red piping on the edges of the collar and cuffs, red cuff flaps, red shoulder straps, and one row of brass buttons; gray riding trousers with red stripes and piping; dark-green forage caps with a likewise dark-green band, red piping, and a leather visor (Illus. 1860). Personnel in non-commissioned officer ranks had gold galloon on the collar and cuffs (Illus. 1860)[155].

5 May 1816 – Officials in the *Military Topographic Depot* that was under the Chief of His Imperial Majesty's Main Staff were prescribed the same uniform as for other officials of this Staff, but with blue [svetlosinii] piping and cuff flaps instead of red (Illus. 1861) [156].

23 June 1821 – *Government craftsmen of the Mechanical establishment [Mekhanicheskoe zavedenie] under His Imperial Majesty's Main Staff*, reorganized from the Machine workshop mentioned above, were assigned the following uniform: single-breasted dark-green frock coat with black collar and (round) cuffs; red shoulder straps, cuff flaps, and piping on the collar, cuffs, and skirt turnbacks; red lining and brass buttons; dark-green pants with red stripes and piping, but of white Flemish linen in summer; dark-green forage caps without visors, with a black band and red piping (Illus. 1862) [157].

9 August 1823 – The *Craftsmen Company of His Imperial Majesty's Main Staff [Masterovaya rota Glavnago Shtaba Ego Imperatorskago Velichestva]*, established at the Court Carriage workshop [Pridvornoe Ekipazhnoe zavedenie], was prescribed the following uniform:

Craftsmen [Masterovye] – dark-green single-breasted tailcoat with blue [svetlosinii] shoulder straps, collar, cuffs, and skirt turnbacks (after the pattern for train personnel), and with white buttons; dark-gray cloth riding trousers with blue stripes and piping, and a thin cord and buttons at the bottom for fastening; gray forage cap with blue band and leather visor and rear piece (Illus. 1863); gray greatcoat with the same shoulder straps, collar, and buttons as on the tailcoat.

Sub-Master Craftsmen [Podmasterya] – the same as for master craftsmen with the addition of silver galloon on the coat's cuffs (Illus. 1864).

Master Craftsmen [Mastera] and *non-commissioned officers* – as for second-level master craftsmen with the addition of silver galloon on the coat's collar (Illus. 1864).

[I confirm the somewhat confusing progression of these ranks from *masterovyi* to *podmaster'* and then to *master* and *unter-ofitser* – M.C.]

Guards, clerks, and *medics* [Vakhtera, pisarya i fel'dshera] – the same as for master craftsmen and non-commissioned officers but instead of the tailcoat a dark-gray single-breasted frock coat with the same collar, cuffs, shoulder straps, and buttons as on the tailcoat (Illus. 1865).

Apart from the above uniforms, all these personnel were authorized winter and summer work clothing of the same patterns as described above in the chapter for Military-Labor battalions [158].

Officers – prescribed the uniform for supply train officers but without shakos [159].

f) Medical personnel.

4 August 1805 – *Medical Sub-Inspectors [Meditsinskie Sub-Inspektory], Chief Staff-Doctors [Glavnye Shtab-Lekarya],* and *Operators [Operatora]*, along with the same uniforms as for regimental doctors, described above under Grenadier regiments, were ordered to have the exact same embroidery on their coat's collar and cuffs as established on 1 February 1808 for 3rd-category military-collegium officials, except in silver instead of gold (Note: this coat was shown previously in Volume X, Illustration No 1263). *Divisional Doctors [Divizionnye Doktora], Chief Doctors of hospitals [Glavnye Doktora gospitalei],* and *General-Staff-Doctors [General-Shtab-Lekarya]* were prescribed embroidery as for the 2nd military-collegium category (Illus. 1866), and the *Chief Medical Inspector for Land Forces [Glavnyi po Voenno-Sukhoputnoi chasti Meditsinskii Inspektor—*as for the 1st category, with persons of rank 5 and higher also authorized plumage on the hat (Illus. 1867) [160].

8 July 1809 – Hat plumage for medical officials of class 5 and higher was removed and the previous buttonhole loop pattern with smooth galloon was replaced with a new one consisting of four thick bullion cords of which the middle two were interwoven together in the form of a plait. About this time medical officials were allowed to wear dark-green pants instead of white for everyday use. They were also given dark-green frock coats with the same buttons and collar as on the tailcoat, but without embroidery [161].

In 1812 – Medical officials began to have collars that were lower than before, closed with small hooks (Illus. 1868) [162].

From 1815 – These officials began to wear hats with white tape around the cockade, later changed to silver [163].

27 March 1818 – *Senior medical orderlies at military hospitals [starshie fel'dshera voennykh gospitalei]* were ordered to wear dark-green single-breasted frock coats with likewise dark-green cuffs (slit) and collar, trimmed with silver galloon, with red piping around the collar, cuffs, and turnbacks, white kersey lining, and white buttons; gray riding trousers without any trim or piping, with seven white buttons on the side seams, but in summer—pants of Flemish linen, with integral spats; dark-green caps with red piping on the crown and band, and a leather visor (Illus. 1869). *Junior medical orderlies [mladshie fel'dshera]* received the same uniform but without galloon (Illus. 1869). *Students [shkol'niki]* being instructed in nursing and orderly duties received a dark-green infantry uniform, also without galloon, with the cuff flaps trimmed around the edges with a red border (Illus. 1870) [164].

g) Veterinary personnel.

3 February 1816 – *Veterinary doctors [veterinarnye lekarya]* were prescribed uniforms similar to those for Army medical officials but with the dark-green coat changed to dark blue *[sinii]*, with a single silver buttonhole loop on the collar and two on each cuff (Illus. 1871). *Veterinary assistants holding officer rank [veterinarnye pomoshchniki ofitserskago china]* were ordered to have the same coats but without buttonhole loops (Illus. 1872), while *veterinary assistants holding non-commissioned officer rank [veterinarnye pomoshchniki unter-ofitserskago zvaniya]* were given dark-blue double-breasted frock coats with red piping and white buttons, blue pants and likewise blue forage caps, with a visor and red piping (Illus. 1872) [165].

h) Apothecary personnel.

27 March 1818 – *Senior apothecary apprentices [starshie aptekarskie ucheniki]* at military hospitals were prescribed the exact same uniform as received at this time by senior hospital orderlies. *Junior apothecary apprentices* received the same but with the addition of dark-green cuff flaps edged in red, as related above for junior hospital orderlies [166].

Russian Artillery 1814

NOTES

(1) *Complete Collection of Laws [Polnoe Sobranie Zakonov, henceforth PSZ]*, Vol. XXVI, pg. 609, No 19,826.

(2) Ibid., Vol. XXIV, Part II, Regulations for uniforms, pg. 73, No 20,109.

(3) Ibid., pg. 30, No 20,186.

(4) Ibid., 73 and 59, No 20,109. and Highest confirmed table of uniforms, accouterments, and weapons for a Garrison battalion on a field establishment, 30 April 1802.

(5) Ditto.

(6) Ditto.

(7) Ditto.

(8) Ibid., pgs. 29 and 30, NoNo 20,109 and 20,186, and the Highest confirmed table referenced above, in appendices 4, 5, 6, and 7.

(9) PSZ Vol. XLIV, pg. 29, No 20,109.

(10) Highest confirmed table of uniforms, accouterments, and weapons for a Garrison battalion on an internal establishment, 30 April 1802.

(11) PSZ Vol. XLIV, pgs. 63 and 64, No 20,287, but the colors for poles and drumsticks remained the same as stated in Vol. IX of this work.

(12) From the Archive files of the War Ministry's Commissariat Department. PSZ Vol. XLIV, pg. 67, No 20,297, and an actual model headdress preserved at the War Ministry's Commissariat Department.

(13) Determination made by the Government Military Collegium, dated 20 October 1803.

(14) PSZ Vol. XXVIII, pg. 415, No 21,377, and statements by contemporaries.

(15) Memorandum from the Government Military Collegium to the War Commission [*Voinskaya Kommissiya*], dated 3 August 1804, and information received from the War Ministry's Commissariat Department.

(16) Memorandum from the Government Military Collegium to the War Commission, dated 31 December 1804.

(17) PSZ Vol. XLIV, pg. 73, No 21,593.

(18) Ibid., pg. 67, No 21,589.

(19) Ibid., No 21,969.

(20) Ibid., pg. 73, No 21,987.

(21) Ibid., pg. 31, No 22,197.

(22) Ibid., pg. 73, NoNo 23,205 and 23,325, and ukases of the Government Collegium for the year 1808.

(23) PSZ Vol. XXIX, pg. 901, No 22,382.

(24) Ibid., pg. 1040, No 22,482.

(25) Ibid., Vol. XLIV, pg. 67, No 22,727.

(26) Ibid., pg. 73, No 22,880.

(27) Ibid., pg. 73, No 23,325.

(28) Ibid., Vol. XXX, pg. 508, No 23,206.

(29) Ibid., Vol. XLIV, pg. 67, No 23,335.

(30) Ibid., Vol. XLIV, pg. 68, No 23,382.

(31) Ibid., pg. 73, No 23,451.

(32) Ibid., Vol. XXX, pg. 781, No 23,478.

(33) Ibid., pg. 950, No 23,623, and the Moscow Section of the Archive of the War Ministry's Inspection Department, file No 13,786/654.

(34) From the Archive of the War Ministry's Commissariat Department.

(35) PSZ Vol. XXX, pg. 904, No 23,571.

(36) Ibid., pg. 950, No 23,625; information received from the War Ministry's Commissariat Department, and an actual model knapsack preserved there.

(37) PSZ Vol. XXX, pg. 1006, No 23,695.

(38) Information received from the War Ministry's Commissariat Department.

(39) PSZ Vol. XLIV, pg. 24, No 23.914.

(40) Ibid., pg. 73, No 24,016.

(41) Statements from contemporaries.

(42) PSZ Vol. XXXI, pg. 362, No 24,357, and information received from the War Ministry's Commissariat Department.

(43) Statements from contemporaries.

(44) PSZ Vol. XLIV, pg. 73, No 24,612, and information received from the War Ministry's Commissariat Department.

(45) PSZ Vol. XXXI, pg. 855, No 27,794.

(46) Ibid., pg. 31, NoNo 24,911 and 24,912, and information received from the War Ministry's Commissariat Department.

(47) Ibid., pg. 70, No 24,991, and information received from the War Ministry's Commissariat Department.

(48) Information received from the same Department, and model items preserved there and in various Arsenals.

(49) PSZ Vol. XLIV, pg. 109, No 26,053.

(50) PSZ Vol. XXXIII, pg. 1014, No 26,426, § 6.

(51) Highest Order announced by the Chief of HIS IMPERIAL MAJESTY's Main Staff to the Minister of War, 8 September 1816, and information received from the War Ministry's Commissariat Department.

(52) Information received from the same Department.

(53) Ditto.

(54) Ditto.

(55) Information received from the War Ministry's Commissariat Department, and PSZ Vol. XLIV, pg. 140, No 20,713.

(56) PSZ Vol. XLIV, pg. 139, No 29,912.

(57) Ibid., pg. 129, No 30,151.

(58) Ibid., pg. 139, No 39,136, and information received from the War Ministry's Commissariat Department.

(59) PSZ Vol. XL, pg. 188, No 30,303.

(60) Ibid., Vol. XLIV, pg. 73, No 24,612; Vol. XXI, pg. 631, No 24,615, and information received from the War Ministry's Commissariat Department.

(61) Highest confirmed table of uniforms, accouterments, and weapons for a battalion of the Internal Guard, 3 July 1811.

(62) PSZ Vol. XLIV, pg. 31, NoNo 24,911 and 24,912.

(63) Ibid., pg. 70, No 24,991, and information received from the War Ministry's Commissariat Department.

(64) Information received from the same Department.

(65) Ditto.

(66) PSZ Vol. XLIV, pg. 139, No 26,272.

(67) HIGHEST Order to the Minister of War, 10 September 1816, No. 386, and information drawn from the files of the War Ministry's Commissariat Department.

(68) HIGHEST confirmed table of 18 May 1817, and information received from the War Ministry's Commissariat Department.

(69) PSZ Vol. XXV, pg. 122, No 27,284; information received from the War Ministry's Commissariat Department; see also the entry for 29 April 1811, above.

(70) Information received from the War Ministry's Commissariat Department.

(71) PSZ Vol. XLIV, pg. 140, No 29,713.

(72) Ibid., Vol. XL, pg. 188, No 30,309.

(73) Ibid., Vol. XLIV, pg. 140, NoNo 26,650 and 28,865; Highest confirmed table of uniforms, accouterments, and weapons for Gendarme battalions and commands, 18 May 1817; information received from the War Ministry's Commissariat Department.

(74) PSZ Vo. XL, pg. 188, No 30,309.

(75) Ibid., Vol. XXVI, pg. 609, No 19,826.

(76) Highest confirmed table of uniforms, accouterments, and weapons for Invalid companies and commands, 30 April 1802.

(77) Information received from the War Ministry's Commissariat Department.

(78) The Highest confirmed table cited above in Note 76.

(79) PSZ Vol. XLIV, pg. 74, No 22,247.

(80) Ibid., Vol. XXIX, pg. 201, No 22,382.

(81) Ibid., Vol. XLIV, pg. 67, No 22,727.

(82) Ibid., pg. 67, No 23,335.

(83) Ibid., pg. 24, No 23,914.

(84) Information drawn from the files of the War Ministry's Commissariat Department.

(85) PSZ Vol. XLIV, pg. 140, No 26,053.

(86) Statements from contemporaries.

(87) HIGHEST Order to the Minister of War, 20 February 1816, No 118.

(88) PSZ Vol. XLIV, pg. 140, No 26,422a.

(89) Ibid., pg. 140, No 27,082.

(90) Ibid., pg. 141, No 27,660.

(91) Ibid., pg. 139 No 29,912.

(92) Ibid., Vol. XL, pg. 188, No 30,309.

(93) Information drawn from the files of the War Ministry's Commissariat Department and the St.-Petersburg Internal Garrison Battalion.

(94) PSZ Vol. XLIV, pg. 140, No 26,053, and Information received from the War Ministry's Commissariat Department.

(95) Statements by contemporaries.

(96) PSZ Vol. XLIV, pg. 139, No 26,272.

(97) Highest Resolution on a report by the Chief of HIS IMPERIAL MAJESTY's Main Staff, 9 June 1817.

(98) PSZ Vol. XLIV, pg. 140, No 20,782.

(99) Signed ukase to the Minister of War, 25 December 1817.

(100) PSZ Vol. XLIV, pg. 141, No 28,921.

(101) Information received from the War Ministry's Commissariat Department.

(102) PSZ Vol. XLIV, pg. 139, No 29,912.

(103) Ibid., Vol. XL, pg. 188, No 30,309.

(104) Information drawn from the files of the War Ministry's Commissariat Department and the Staff of the Separate Corps of the Internal Guard.

(105) PSZ Vol. XLIV, pg. 140, No 28,156.

(106) Information received from the War Ministry's Commissariat Department.

(107) PSZ Vol. XXXIII, pg. 1091, No 26,517.

(108) Ibid., Vol. XLIV, pg. 140, No 27,127.

(109) Ibid., pg. 140, No 27,422.

(110) Order of the Commander-in-Chief of military settlements, 5 November 1823, point 4.

(111) PSZ Vol. XXVI, pg. 609, No 19,826.

(112) Ibid., Vol. XXIX, pg. 201, No 22,832.

(113) Ibid., Vol. XLIV, pg. 29, No 23,859.

(114) Highest Resolution on a report by the Chief of HIS IMPERIAL MAJESTY's Main Staff, 10 March 1816.

(115) PSZ Vol. XXXIII, pg. 1091, No 26,517, and information drawn from the files of the Archive of the Department of Military Settlements.

(116) PSZ Vol. XLIV, pg. 122, No 26,986, and model uniform clothing of 15 August 1817, preserved at the War Ministry's Commissariat Department.

(117) Information receieved from this Department.

(118) PSZ Vol. XLIV, pg. 140, No 27,127, and information drawn from the files of the Archive of the Department of Military Settlements.

(119) Order of the Commander-in-Chief of military settlements, 30 December 1818.

(120) Order of the same, 16 June 1819.

(121) *Collection of Laws and Directives Relating to Military Administration*[*Sobranie Zakonov i postanovlenii, do chasti Voennago upravleniya otnosyashchikhsya*], 1821, Book III, pgs. 251 and 7.

(122) Order of the Commander-in-Chief of military settlements, 21 October 1821.

(123) PSZ Vol. XXVI, pg. 609, No 19,826.

(124) Ibid., Vol. XXIX, pg. 901, No 22,382.

(125) Ibid., Vol. XLIV, Sect. IV. Reign of Emperor AlexanderI, pg. 224.

(126) Ibid., Vol. XLIV, Sect. IV. Regulations on uniforms, pg. 74, No 22,578, and statements from contemporaries.

(127) Ditto.

(128) Ibid., pg. 85, No 23,262.

(129) Ibid., pgs. 85 and 86, No 23,764.

(130) Model uniform for these battalions, preserved at the War Ministry's Commissariat Department.

(131) PSZ Vol. XXX, pg. 273, No 20,036, and Vol. XXXIII, pg. 879, No 26,301.

(132) Ditto.

(133) Ibid., Vol. XXX, pg. 1043, No 23,756.

(134) Ibid., Vol. XXII, pg. 377, No 25,166.

(135) Ibid., pg. 391, No 25,179.

(136) Ibid., Vol. XXXIII, pgs. 878 et seq., No 26,301.

(137) Ibid., Vol. XXIV, pg. 32, No 19,781.

(138) Ibid., Vol. XXVII, pg. 35, No 20,130.

(139) Ibid., Vol. XLIV, pg. 32, No 20,184.

(140) Information received from the War Ministry's Commissariat Department.

(141) PSZ Vol. XXIX, pg. 394, No 22,188.

(142) Ibid., Vol. XLIV, pg. 33, No 22,805, and model coats preserved at the War Ministry's Commissariat Department.

(143) PSZ Vol. XLIV, pg. 33, No 22,822.

(144) Ibid., pg. 33, No 22,860.

(145) Ibid., Vol. XXX, pg. 106, No 22,864.

(146) Information received from the War Ministry's Commissariat Department.

(147) PSZ Vol. XXVII, pg. 507, No 20,678.

(148) Information received from the War Ministry's Commissariat Department, and a model frock coat preserved there.

(149) Statements by contemporaries.

(150) PSZ Vol. XLIV, pg. 122, No 26,190a.

(151) Model uniform preserved at the War Ministry's Commissariat Department.

(152) PSZ Vol. XLIV, pg. 122, No 26,637.

(153) PSZ Vol. XLIII, Part II, Book of Establishment Tables, continuation of First Section, pgs. 403 and 404, No 24,744, and Information received from the War Ministry's Commissariat Department.

(154) PSZ Vol. XLIII, No 24,942.

(155) Highest Confirmed description of uniform clothing for personnel of HIS IMPERIAL MAJESTY's Main Staff, 12 February 1816.

(156) Highest Confirmed report by the Chief of HIS IMPERIAL MAJESTY's Main Staff, 5 May 1816.

(157) PSZ Vol. XLIII, Part II, Book of Establishment Tables, continuation of First Section, pgs. 152 and 153, and information received from the War Ministry's Commissariat Department.

(158) Ibid., pg. 21, No 29,578.

(159) Ibid., Vol. XXXVIII, pg. 1163, No 29578, § 22.

(160) Ibid., XXIV, pg. 31, No 22,197, and statements by contemporaries.

(161) Statements by contemporaries.

(162) Ditto.

(163) Ditto.

(164) PSZ Vol. XLIV, pg. 121, and model uniform clothing preserved at the War Ministry's Commissariat Department.

(165) PSZ Vol. XXXIII, pg. 472, No 26,121, §§ 11, 12, and 13.

(166) PSZ Vol. XLIV, pg. 121, No 27,321, and model uniform clothing preserved at the War Ministry's Commissariat Department.

РИСУНКИ
ОДЕЖДЫ и ВООРУЖЕНІЯ
РОССІЙСКИХЪ
ВОЙСКЪ
1801-1825.

PLATES LIST OF ILLUSTRATIONS

1824. Private. District Invalid Commands, 1811-1815.

1825. Drummer and Company-Grade Officer. Serving District Invalid Commands, 1811-1815.

1826. Private. Serving District Invalid Commands, 1817-1824.

1827. Field-Grade Officer. Non-Serving District Invalid Commands, 1822-1823.

1828. Private. District Invalid Commands, 1824-1825.

1829. Private and Non-Commissioned Officer. Invalid Commands with Settled Grenadier Regiments, 1816-1825.

1830. Non-Serving Invalid. Setteled Lancer Regiments, 1811-1823.

1831. Non-Serving Invalid. Setteled Lancer Regiments, 1818-1823.

1832. Military Cantonist. Settled Grenadier Regiments, 1816-1825.

1833. Pupil. Military Orphans' Sections, 1817-1825.

1834. Military Cantonist. Settled Lancer Regiments, 1817-1821.

1835. Military Cantonists. Instructional Squadrons of Settled Lancer Regiments and Instructional Battalions of Settled Grenadier Regiments, 1821-1825.

1836. Privates. Provincial Companies and State Commands, 1807-1808.

1837. Privates. Provincial Companies and State Commands of St.-Petersburg and Voronezh Provinces, 1809-1811.

1838. Privates. Provincial Companies and State Commands of Penza, Poltava, and Kherson Provinces, 1809-1811.

1839. NCO Provincial Companies and State Commands of Vitebsk and Georgia Provinces, 1809-1811.

1840. Drummers. Provincial Companies and State Commands of Smolensk and Ryazan Provinces, 1809-1811.

1841. Private and Non-Commissioned Officer. Mines Battalions, 1820-25.

1842. Company-Grade Officer. Mines Battalions, 1820-1825.

1843. Recruit. 1808-1812.

1844. Recruit. 1812-1816.

1845. Recruits. 1816-1825.

1846. Chancellery Employee. Government Military Collegium, 1802-1809.

1847. Official. Government Military Collegium, 1802-1803.

1848. Coat Embroidery for Personnel of the Gov.Military Collegium. (Established 7 February 1808. 1st Category.)

1849. Member. Government Military Collegium, 1808-1809.

1850. Coat Embroidery for Personnel of the Gov. Military Collegium. (Established 1 February 1808. 2nd Category.)

1851. Official. Government Military Collegium, 1808-1811. (2nd Category.)

1852. Officials. Government Military Collegium, 1808-1811. (3rd and 4th Categories.)

1853. Chancellery Employee. Government Military Collegium, 1809-1811.

1854. Member. Government Military Collegium, 1809-1811.

1855. Officials. War Ministry, 1812-1815.

1856. Commissariat and Provisioning Departments of the War Ministry, 1816-1825.

1857. Employee at the General Staff Building, 1811-1812.

1858. Government Master Craftsman [Masterovyi]. Machine Workshop at the General Staff Building, 1812-21.

1859. Officials. Main Staff, 1816-1825.

1860. Clerks. H.I.M. Main Staff, 1816-1825.

1861. Clerk and Official. Military Topographic Depot of H.I.M. Main Staff, 1816-1825.

1862. Government Craftsman. The Mechanical Establishment of H.I.M. Main Staff, 1821-25.

1863. Craftsman. Craftsmen Company of H.I.M. Main Staff, 1823-25.

1864. Sub- Master Craftsman and Master Craftsman [Master]. Craftsmen Company of H.I.M. Main Staff, 1823-25.

1865. Guard. Craftsmen Company of H.I.M. Main Staff, 1823-25.

1866. Chief Doctor. Military Hospitals, 1805-1812.

1867. Chief Medical Inspector for Land Forces, 1805-1809.

1868. Chief Staff-Doctor. 1812-1825.

1869. Senior and Junior Medical Orderlies. Military Hospitals, 1818-1825. (In winter and summer uniform.)

1870. Student in nursing and orderly duties, 1818-1825.

1871. Veterinary Doctor, 1816-1825.

1872. Veterinary Assistants. Company-Grade Officer and Non-Commmissioned Officer Ranks, 1816-1825.

Private. Garrisons of the Finland Inspectorate, 1802-1803

1774

Non-Commissioned Officer. Garrisons of the St.Petersburg Inspectorate, 1802-1803

Non-Commissioned Officer. Garrisons of the Lifland Inspectorate, 1802-1803

1776

Company Drummer. Garrisons of the Dniester Inspectorate, 1802-1803

Battalion Drummer. Garrisons of the Caucasus Inspectorate, 1802-1803

Company-Grade Officer. Garrisons of the Smolensk Inspectorate, 1802-1803

1779

Field-Grade Officer. Garrisons of the Kiev Inspectorate, 1802-1803

General. Garrisons of the Moscow Inspectorate, 1802-1803

Train Personnel. Garrisons of the Orenburg Inspectorate, 1802-1803

Clerk. Garrisons of the Siberia Inspectorate, 1802-1803

Field-Grade Officer and Drummer. Garrisons of the Dnieper Inspectorate, 1804-1806

Privates. Garrison Regiments and Battalions, 1806-1807

Privates. Garrison Regiments and Battalions, 1808-1809

Company-Grade Officers. Garrison Regiments and Battalions, 1808-1810

Train Personnel. Garrison Regiments and Battalions, 1809-1811

Private and Company-Grade Officer. Kazan Garrison Regiment, 1811-1812

NCO. Garrison Regiments and Battalions, 1811

Company-Grade Officer and Private. Garrison Regiments and Battalions, 1812-1815

Drummer and Company-Grade Officer. Garrison Regiments and Battalions, 1816-1823

Field-Grade Officer and Private. Garrison Regiments and Battalions, 1824-1825

Private. Orenburg Garrison Regiment, 1824-1825

Musician. Archangel Garrison Regiment, 1824-1825

Non-Commissioned Officers. Battalions and Half-Battalions of the Internal Guard, 1811-1812.

Privates. Battalions and Half-Battalions of the Internal Guard, 1811-1812

Field-Grade Officers. Battalions and Half-Battalions of the Internal Guard, 1811-1812

1798

Field-Grade Officer and Non-Commissioned Officer.　　　　　　　　Battalions and Half-Battalions of the Inter-

nal Guard, 1812-1816

Drummer. Battalions of the Internal Guard, 1816

Field-Grade Officer. Battalions of the Internal Guard, 1816-1822

Private and Non-Commissioned Officer. Battalions of the Internal Guard, 1817-1825

Company and Field-Grade Officers. Battalions of the Internal Guard, 1823

1803

Private. Battalions of the Internal Guard, 1824-1825

Private. Gendarme Battalions, 1817-1825

Non-Commissioned Officer. Gendarme Battalions, 1817-1825

Trumpeter. Gendarme Battalions, 1817-1825

Field-Grade Officer. Gendarme Battalions, 1817-1825

Private. Gendarme Commands, 1817-1825

Non-Commissioned Officer. Gendarme Commands, 1817-1825

Private. Invalid Companies, 1802-1806

Non-Commissioned Officer. Invalid Companies, 1802-1806

Drummer. Invalid Companies, 1802-1806

Company-Grade Officer. Invalid Companies, 1802-1806

Private. Invalid Companies and Commands, 1806

Private. Invalid Companies with Garrison Regiments and Battalions, 1807-1811

Drummer. Invalid Companies with Garrison Regiments and Battalions, 1807-1811

Non-Commissioned Officer and Private. Mobile Invalid Companies, 1811-1815

Drummer. Mobile Invalid Companies, 1811-1815

1819

Company-Grade Officer. Mobile Invalid Companies, 1811-1815

Company-Grade Officer and Private. Mobile Invalid Companies, 1816

Private. Mobile Invalid Companies, 1817-1824

Private. Reserve Mobile Invalid Companies, 1819-1824

Drummer. Mobile Invalid Companies, 1824-1825

1824

Private. District Invalid Commands, 1811-1815

Drummer and Company-Grade Officer. Serving District Invalid Commands, 1811-1815

1826

Private. Serving District Invalid Commands, 1817-1824

89

Field-Grade Officer. Non-Serving District Invalid Commands, 1822-1823

Private. District Invalid Commands, 1824-1825

Private and Non-Commissioned Officer.　　　　　　　　　　　　　　*Invalid Commands with Settled*

Grenadier Regiments, 1816-1825.

Non-Serving Invalid. Setteled Lancer Regiments, 1811-1823

Non-Serving Invalid. Setteled Lancer Regiments, 1818-1823

Military Cantonist. Settled Grenadier Regiments, 1816-1825

Pupil. Military Orphans' Sections, 1817-1825

1834

Military Cantonist. Settled Lancer Regiments, 1817-1821

Military Cantonists. Instructional Squadrons of Settled Lancer Regiments and Instructional Battalions of Settled Grenadier Regiments, 1821-1825

1836

Privates. Provincial Companies and State Commands, 1807-1808

Privates. Provincial Companies and State Commands of St.-Petersburg and Voronezh Provinces, 1809-1811

Privates. Provincial Companies and State Commands of Penza, Poltava, and Kherson Provinces, 1809-1811

Non-Commissioned Officers. Provincial Companies and State Commands of Vitebsk and Georgia Provinces, 1809-1811

1840

Drummers. Provincial Companies and State Commands of Smolensk and Ryazan Provinces, 1809-1811

Private and Non-Commissioned Officer. Mines Battalions, 1820-25

Company-Grade Officer. Mines Battalions, 1820-1825

Recruit. 1808-1812

Recruit. 1812-1816

Recruits. 1816-1825

Chancellery Employee. Government Military Collegium, 1802-1809

Official. Government Military Collegium, 1802-1803

Coat Embroidery for Personnel of the Government Military Collegium

1849

Member. Government Military Collegium, 1808-1809

. *Coat Embroidery for Personnel of the Government Military Collegium*

Official. Government Military Collegium, 1808-1811. (2nd Category)

Officials. Government Military Collegium, 1808-1811. (3rd and 4th Categories)

1853

Chancellery Employee. Government Military Collegium, 1809-1811

1854

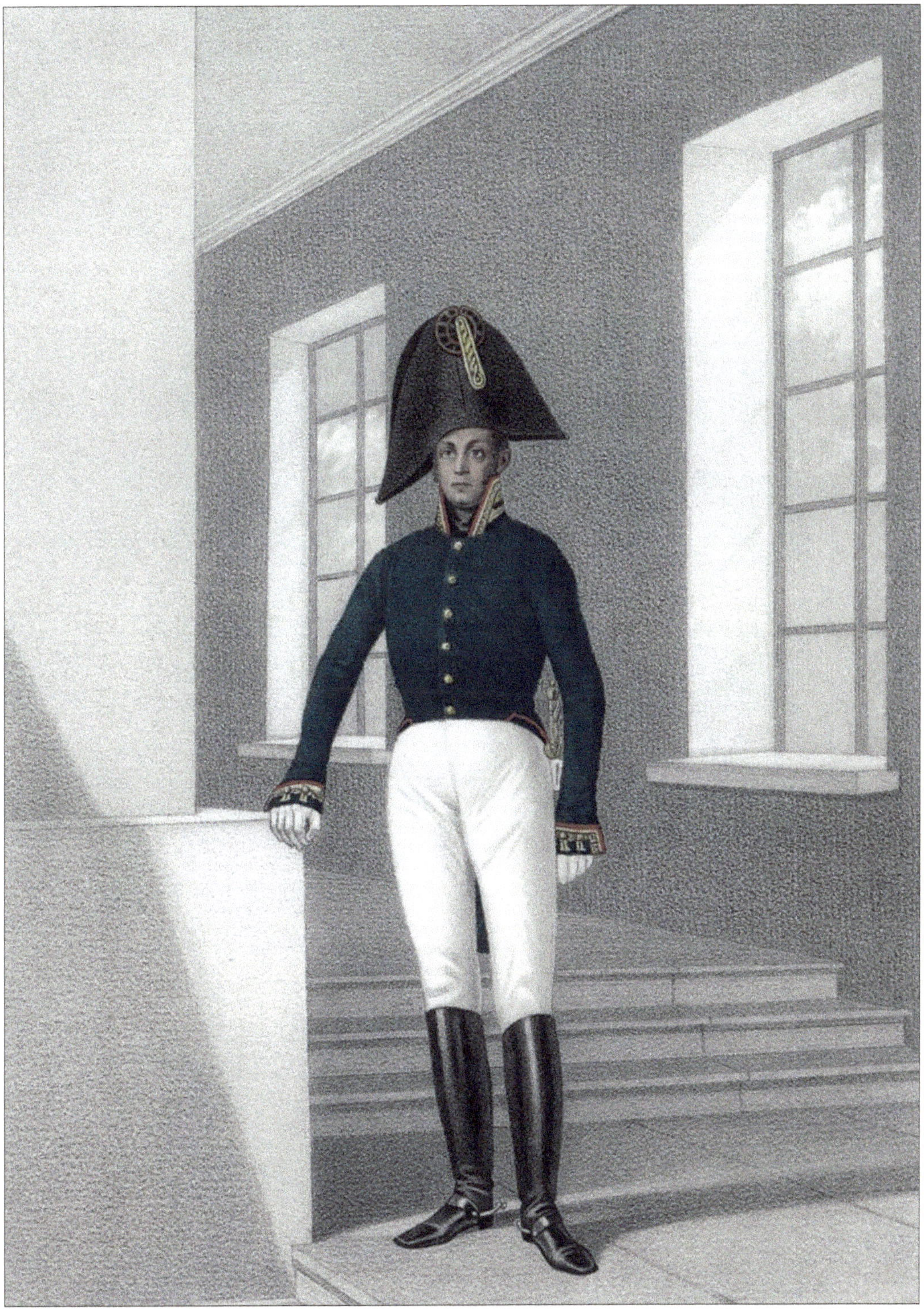

Member. Government Military Collegium, 1809-1811

Officials. War Ministry, 1812-1815

Commissariat and Provisioning Departments of the War Ministry, 1816-1825

Employee at the General Staff Building, 1811-1812

1858

Government Master Craftsman [Masterovyi]. Machine Workshop at the General Staff Building, 1812-21

Officials. Main Staff, 1816-1825

Clerks. H.I.M. Main Staff, 1816-1825

Clerk and Official. Military Topographic Depot of H.I.M. Main Staff, 1816-1825

Government Craftsman. The Mechanical Establishment of H.I.M. Main Staff, 1821-25

Craftsman. Craftsmen Company of H.J.M. Main Staff, 1823-25

Sub- Master Craftsman[Podmaster'] and Master Craftsman [Master].　　　　　　*Craftsmen Company of H.I.M. Main Staff,*

1823-25

Guard. Craftsmen Company of H.J.M. Main Staff, 1823-25

Chief Doctor. Military Hospitals, 1805-1812

Chief Medical Inspector for Land Forces, 1805-1809

Chief Staff-Doctor. 1812-1825

Senior and Junior Medical Orderlies. Military Hospitals, 1818-1825. (In winter and summer uniform.)

Student in nursing and orderly duties, 1818-1825

Veterinary Doctor, 1816-1825

Veterinary Assistants. Company-Grade Officer and Non-Commmissioned Officer Ranks, 1816-1825

SOLDIERS, WEAPONS & UNIFORMS ALREADY PUBLISHED
(SOME TITLES)

UNIFORMS OF RUSSIAN ARMY IN THE ERA OF ANCIENT TZAR
FROM THE REIGN OF VASILI IV TO MICHAEL I, ALEXIS, FEODOR III DURING THE XVII th CENTURY
A.V.VISKOVATOV   LUCA STEFANO CRISTINI
SWU-600-004

UNIFORMS OF RUSSIAN ARMY OF PETER I THE GREAT
FROM THE REIGN OF PETER I TO CATHERINE I, PEER II, ANNA AND IVAN VI. 1682-1741
A.V.VISKOVATOV   LUCA STEFANO CRISTINI
SWU-700-006

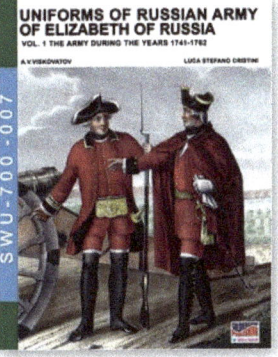

UNIFORMS OF RUSSIAN ARMY OF ELIZABETH OF RUSSIA
VOL. 1 THE ARMY DURING THE YEARS 1741-1762
A.V.VISKOVATOV   LUCA STEFANO CRISTINI
SWU-700-007

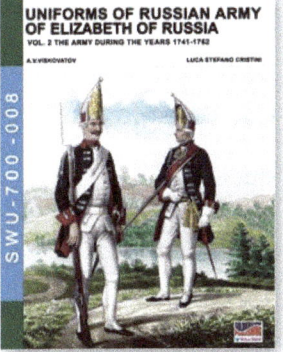

UNIFORMS OF RUSSIAN ARMY OF ELIZABETH OF RUSSIA
VOL. 2 THE ARMY DURING THE YEARS 1741-1762
A.V.VISKOVATOV   LUCA STEFANO CRISTINI
SWU-700-008

UNIFORMS OF RUSSIAN ARMY IN THE XVIII CENTURY VOL. 1
UNDER THE REIGN OF CATHERINE II EMPRESS OF RUSSIA BETWEEN 1762 AND 1796
A.V.VISKOVATOV - LUCA STEFANO CRISTINI
SWU-700-005

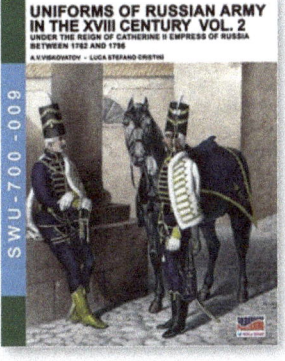

UNIFORMS OF RUSSIAN ARMY IN THE XVIII CENTURY VOL. 2
UNDER THE REIGN OF CATHERINE II EMPRESS OF RUSSIA BETWEEN 1762 AND 1796
A.V.VISKOVATOV - LUCA STEFANO CRISTINI
SWU-700-009

UNIFORMS OF RUSSIAN ARMY IN THE XVIII CENTURY VOL. 3
UNDER THE REIGN OF CATHERINE II EMPRESS OF RUSSIA BETWEEN 1762 AND 1796
A.V.VISKOVATOV - LUCA STEFANO CRISTINI
SWU-700-010

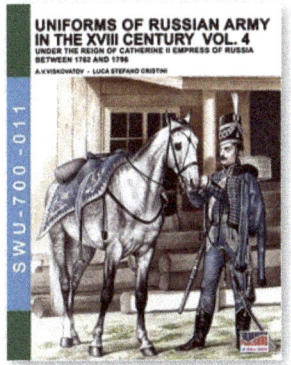

UNIFORMS OF RUSSIAN ARMY IN THE XVIII CENTURY VOL. 4
UNDER THE REIGN OF CATHERINE II EMPRESS OF RUSSIA BETWEEN 1762 AND 1796
A.V.VISKOVATOV - LUCA STEFANO CRISTINI
SWU-700-011

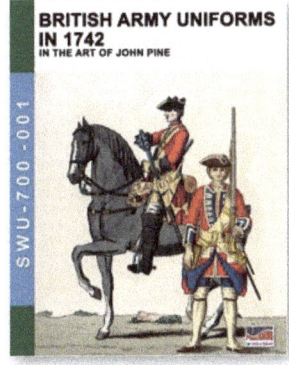

BRITISH ARMY UNIFORMS IN 1742
IN THE ART OF JOHN PINE
SWU-700-001

PRUSSIAN & AUSTRIAN ARMY UNIFORMS IN 1742-1770
LUCA STEFANO CRISTINI
SWU-700-002

THE FRENCH ARMY OF ANCIEN RÉGIME Volume 1
IN THE ART OF FELIX PHILIPPOTEAUX
LUCA STEFANO CRISTINI
SWU-700-003

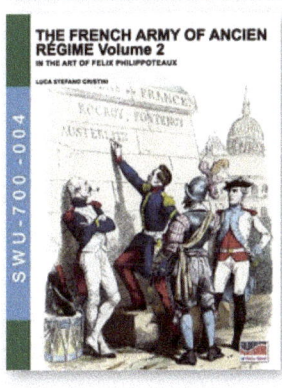

THE FRENCH ARMY OF ANCIEN RÉGIME Volume 2
IN THE ART OF FELIX PHILIPPOTEAUX
LUCA STEFANO CRISTINI
SWU-700-004

THE EXERCISE OF ARMES
JACOB DE GHEYN II - LUCA S. CRISTINI
SWU-600-001

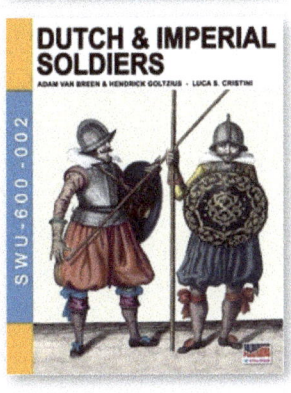

DUTCH & IMPERIAL SOLDIERS
ADAM VAN BREEN & HENDRICK GOLTZIUS - LUCA S. CRISTINI
SWU-600-002

HORSEMEN IN THE 16TH & 17TH C.
JACOB DE GHEYN II - A.DE BRUYN - LUCA S. CRISTINI
SWU-600-003

IMPERIAL SOLDIERS & UNIFORMS 1640-1860
IN THE ART OF FRANZ GERASCH
LUCA S.CRISTINI
Plates by FRANZ GERASCH
SWU-GEN-001

www.ingramcontent.com/pod-product-compliance
Lightning Source LLC
Chambersburg PA
CBHW041142120626
46547CB00020B/3078